A BOOK ABOUT PARIS

"The Revolution's own street of St. Antoine"

A BOOK ABOUT PARIS

By

GEORGE & PEARL ADAM

*

With pictures by

H. FRANKS WARING

JONATHAN CAPE
THIRTY BEDFORD SQUARE LONDON

FIRST PUBLISHED IN MCMXXVII
MADE & PRINTED IN GREAT BRITAIN
BY BUTLER & TANNER LTD
FROME AND
LONDON

CONTENTS

LIST OF ILLUSTRATIONS

INTRODUCTORY

INTRODUCTORY

A CITY SELDOM CHANGES, IT GROWS; AND SOMETIMES IN ITS growth different strains make strange encounters, arousing thought upon Why and Whither, When and How?

The meeting of Le Nôtre and the Roi Soleil, Badinguet and Haussmann, with the Third Republic and the Unknown, at the Arc de Triomphe, provides a whole dish for reflection – Le Nôtre, linking up through the Champs Elysées, a palace destroyed by Communist 'petroleuses' with another palace where the birth and death of the German Empire were acclaimed; victory and disgrace flowing under the Arch; the unhappy Badinguet and his Haussmann; Napoleon for ever marching towards the dimmed Etoile of his fate. And now, interrupted first by 1870 and then by 1914, the last Haussmann artery has joined Louis' 'Grands Boulevards.' Republican Paris has completed what the Second Empire of Shoddy and Magnificence began. Prosaic municipal councillors, anonymous architects and town-planners, are carrying on the work hitherto signed by Emperors and History; and the ramparts of Paris are being replaced by a ring of playing-fields and gardens which will form the last of the real boulevards.

Paris is like a lake into which a large stone has been cast. Fishermen settling on the Ile de la Cité formed the first ripple on the lake when they built a stake palisade for their protection. Since then, as the city spread, its outgrown circles of ramparts have become boulevards, and now the last ripple is swelling up to be petrified in the twenty-six kilometre ring of new boulevards.

The defences of Paris now lie upon the country's frontiers, and although thoroughfares will still be christened boulevards, they will be masqueraders without a soul and without tradition; mere products of the surveyor's theodolitic era.

Economic and traffic considerations to-day dictate the future of Paris. When Haussmann started to plan his monument to Napoleon III there were just over a million inhabitants in Paris. Life was leisurely. The *fiacre* and the three-horsed *impériale*, with its red-waistcoated, cockaded driver, jogged comfortably about the city. Fine *équipages* flashed up and down the Champs Elysées. There was room in which to live, air to breathe, and time for the enjoyment of life.

13

To-day there are some four million Parisians who are whirled about underground, overhead, in train, tram, tube, bus and motor-car, with such rapidity that unhappy traffic and town-planning experts must sometimes suspect them of having solved the problem of being in several places at the same time. Paris has outgrown her strength. Her broadest avenues are too narrow to accommodate her traffic, and one-way streets, gyratory movements, traffic towers, bells and lights, are only palliatives of the dread disease of centralization from which she suffers.

The now disappearing ramparts have had a hypnotic effect like that of a white chalk-line upon a hen. Many of the suburban trams still turn out their passengers at the city gates, and it is only since 1923 that any Paris bus has ventured into the cold world that lies beyond Parisian municipal limits. No pioneering pickaxe has dared to burrow underneath that white line, and all underground railways pull up short at the invisible barrier. Despite the inconvenience thus occasioned, Paris is surrounded, especially on the west, by large overflow towns. People are being forced away from Paris to the suburbs, and the abolition of ramparts and of *octroi* will considerably hasten the exodus. The general trend is westward. It is shown clearly in the rapid migration of fashion from the Grands Boulevards towards the Étoile. While the Rue de la Paix retains its distinction as a fashionable lounge and millionaire's shopping centre, the grands boulevards, once the parade-ground of elegance, have completely surrendered to the cheap-jack, pedlars of false pearls, cinemas and banks. Of cafés of character, not one remains. Good restaurants have practically vanished. Gone is the Jockey Club; the touristocrat and the plutocrat have ousted the aristocrats, and even the plebeian Parisian has to fight hard for room on his own boulevard between the Madeleine and the Rue de la Chaussée d'Antin.

Fortunately French character has so far proved too strong to be much affected by foreign invasion. Life in real Paris remains unchanged; but if you want to find a Parisian, you are certainly more likely to be successful if you look round the Place de la Bastille and the Faubourg Saint-Antoine than you would be at Montmartre or

14

the Etoile. In real Paris all the 'bistros' are not American bars, and blue jeans and baggy velveteens still are worn. Old senators continue to sip their brandy at Foyot's, and French children still play round the 'bassin' of the Luxembourg gardens. The Sorbonne goes on looking more like a penal settlement than a great seat of learning. Coster-merchants of the Four Seasons still push their barrows through the streets. Chair-menders tootle on their brass horns. But the hand of change is on it all. The cry of the chair-mender is heard more and more faintly through the roar of the motor. The coster is being chased by the police to quiet streets where he must die. Slowly, but surely, the inhabitant himself is being driven out, for even the noise-loving Parisian can no longer withstand the vast din that rises up day and night from the centre of the town. The molten lava of Montmartre has flowed down from the mountain along the Rue Caumartin and the Rue Daunou, offending even the dignity of the Rue de la Paix.

*   *   *   *   *

Real Paris, which is unknown to the crowd of cosmopolitan snobs who flatter themselves that they are the 'vrais Parisiens,' still persists and expands, choked here and there by exotic weeds, hampered everywhere by post-war troubles. More than ever before is she the unquestioned political, intellectual and industrial capital. While she remains the great pageant-field of France, she can be as drab as any other industrial town; that she can also be much more brilliant than most is due to accumulated traditions of splendour and romance, of taste, of art and of fashion, and not to any special quality of frivolity among her inhabitants. Nothing less frivolous-minded than the Parisian tinker, tailor and candlestick-maker could well be found. Nor can the Civil Servants, bank-clerks, shop-assistants, anaemic midinettes, factory hands, old noblesse, be regarded as frivolous, in view of the conditions of their lives. Thrift and frivolity do not usually go together. The Parisian is light-hearted. He lives harder, more vividly than does the Londoner. He works more, and derives more enjoyment out of his play.

*   *   *   *   *

15

An unfailing sign of the grave spirit in which a man takes life is his readiness to risk it for an idea or an emotion. In that the Parisian has never shown himself frivolous. He may have sung on Revolution's barricades, bowed ironically when he met Dr. Guillotin, but he has gone forth gallantly even for his disbeliefs. He has lived thriftily and died extravagantly, and many are the monuments to his end. The stones of the Pont de la Concorde were quarried in the blood of the Bastille. The Arc de Triomphe, graven with a hundred names of battles where raw conscript, 'Marie-Louise,' and scarred old *grognard* fell together, covers with its shade the symbol of the latest sacrifice of the 'frivolous' French to their elusive and unsatisfactory Trinity: 'Liberté, Egalité, Fraternité.'

B

1: THE SPINE

NO BUILDING IN AN OLD CITY CAN BE AS ROMANTIC AS ITS ROAD-ways, although few thoughts are given to them. It is roads which build cities, and you turn to right or left to-day to visit some famous cathedral or royal dwelling because a thousand years ago pilgrims walking to Rome from England or Flanders followed the easiest path; and it had been made by a shepherd five hundred years earlier; and he had chosen it because half a thousand years earlier a palace fell into ruins, and stone slabs make good going for shepherds and their flocks; and the Romans built those palaces along a track already centuries-deep in similar histories. Your taxi flies hooting over the path Erasmus trod when he came to Paris; and Erasmus walked through busy, noisy streets where once the Emperor Julian paced his garden-walks, and looked forth over his 'dear Lutetia,' perhaps reflecting on its growth since Julius Caesar there assembled a conference of the Gauls four hundred years before.

In spite of Baron Haussmann's brutal ruler, with which he tried to bring the streets of Paris into line with the points of the compass, the roadways of the city are still eloquent, and you can take a bus-ride from one railway station to another through the Middle Ages.

The first Paris road was her river; it is still a busy one. The Seine gathers in so many other rivers, is connected with so many even greater ones, that the original Paris island was a sort of Clapham Junction of Commerce. First came fish, from many streams; then fishermen, with their wattle huts; then distributors of fish throughout the neighbourhood; new roads for them; a market; a band of merchants, the sails of whose boats are still the arms of a town two hundred and thirty-three miles inland; soldiers to protect them; then trade and defence ever interacting, and bringing after them learning, the arts, prosperity, aggression, resistance, all the confusion of a place which is growing because it is prosperous, and is fighting because it is coveted.

There are few buildings left in Paris to recall these stages of its life – a bit of wall, a tower, the Roman Emperor's bath-house, or the arena where men fought with beasts, as at Ephesus, and the citizens paid to see it, as at Wonderland. Only the roads remain; and not even the enlightened town-planner has managed to erase their significance from the map of Paris.

The Boulevard Saint-Michel, which swallowed many ancient streets, draws a straight efficient line down the hill; but to the east of it, its feet in Antwerp and Canterbury, and its head in Rome, runs the Rue Saint-Jacques. It is sometimes ample, sometimes narrow. There are places in it whence one looks down a wide perspective of impressively modern, impressively uniform, impressively dull University buildings. There are other portions where the tall ancient houses lean forward arm-in-arm, like shaky old people dancing Sir Roger de Coverley, leaving barely space for one couple to totter down the middle.

It runs through Roman Paris, mediaeval Paris, Reformation and Renaissance Paris; down the hill from which Julian looked out and Sainte Geneviève watched her city, to the river; and beside it has grown a thick hedge of monuments to human wishes and hopes.

The names of Roman emperor and mediaeval shepherdess-saint are perpetuated in palace and church. The faith that brought men barefoot across Europe in single crusades of the lonely human soul, and built monasteries to house them, has left its mark in street-name, fountain and wall. The thirst for knowledge that from the ashes of Rome brought forth Italy, mother of knowledge and beauty, after one thousand years of hatching in the monasteries, made the Sorbonne, and its cluster of national colleges.

Some of these still exist. They had never heard of swimming-baths and laundries, such as are boasted by our 'Cité Universitaire,' which we think so modern; the Montsouris quarter was to them merely one portion of the country-side upon the road to Rome; but they knew something about how to lodge compatriot students cheaply and efficiently; and there a few yet stand, crumbling with bewilderment, but quite sure that the unfatigued Sorbonne is still their natural centre.

Where the feet of men pass, and the minds of men pause, there must men be fed. Even to this day, when modern transport has enabled the student to live farther away from the Sorbonne, in airier

"The first Paris road was her river"

streets and lighter rooms, the Rue Saint-Jacques has many small eating-houses, stuffy and noisy, but – cardinal virtue – cheap. In the old days, food, learning and religion divided it between them: Anatole France placed la Rôtisserie de la Reine Pedauque in the Rue Saint-Jacques. (A new hostelry of the same name is now flourishing in the modern Paris which reads Anatole France; there is admirable fare there, but no Jerôme Coignard.)

Rue pépinière

This was the road where Roman soldiers marched clashing to their outpost of Empire. On this highway walked monks, duffle-clad, when many centuries had grassed the tomb of Rome; some with a crucifix hurting their breast; some with a bottle (thieved from last night's inn) in their pockets; some with both. Hence went forth the Crusaders on their way to rescue the Holy Tomb, and by this road they brought back after years their battered bodies and their new notions of civilization. And, centuries later, here came students, as hopefully as pilgrims, to find the learning which was to redeem a world that would not be redeemed by holiness; only to discover that, two thousand five hundred years earlier, a Jewish King had known that in much wisdom is much grief and that he that increaseth knowledge increaseth sorrow. Along this road went Saint Louis, to fetch from Sens the Crown of Thorns, that it might be saved from pawning by the sacrilegious Baldwin of Constantinople, and housed by this same wayside in that loveliest of shrines, the Sainte-Chapelle.

The road slopes down to the river, and there meets the Petit Pont. The first Paris is like a ship anchored with her nose down-stream, and the bridges from the banks to the Ile de la Cité are so many gangways leading to the Admiral's deck. The Petit Pont was a very unhappy gangway; it was swept away eleven times by floods in five centuries. The last time it burned as well. As it was in each case heavily burdened with living-houses, these were catastrophes not to be forgotten. At last Napoleon III had the idea of making a bridge which would continue, and in 1853 one stone arch was thrown over that branch of the river. But the Romans, the Crusaders, the pilgrims, the students, crossed very rough planking, with crazy wooden cliffs of houses on either hand; and in every window the rosy-faced girl who waved them on their way would blanch suddenly, even as she smiled, if a weight of water or a block of ice struck suddenly upon the supports of this amphibious highway. Once, upon St. Crispin's Day, about half-past nine on a bright morning, all the arches and all the houses and all the inhabitants and all the passers-by slid into the river. One baby, in a wicker cradle, floated and survived.

The landsmen set foot upon this ship-island, and found it as self-contained as any battleship; dependent, like them, upon the main-land for revictualling and refuelling, but complete from flag to chaplain, manned by a highly-trained crew of specialists, and exercising upon the adjacent countries and their hinterlands an influence as imperious as Caesar's.

As in a ship, all the necessary activities of life were concentrated; and, for lack of space, they had to be as sharply defined in their limits as the bridge, the ward-room and the gun-room. The King lived, and justice was administered, upon the left, where lay also the Crown of Thorns in its exquisite chapel. Close by were the lodgings of the Crusaders, situated in streets called Galilee, Nazareth, or Jeru-salem, after the holy places they were to visit or had left – streets which were to see the births of two such widely-contrasted men as Boileau and Voltaire. Your altar and your priests were on the right; and the warriors, swaggering free-thinkers, but very superstitious, were housed near by. Kings and Crusaders are no more; but God, Law and the Army are still housed where they were; the Ile de la Cité is to this day as definite as a beehive in its departments, as busy in its traffic, and as useful in its activity.

The religion of France has its centre upon the spot where, under the cathedral of Notre-Dame de Paris, was found, not so very long ago, an altar to Jupiter, on which lay the wood-ash of the last sacrifice made in his honour before his temple fell and the bells of the Christians began to sound along this valley.

The justice of France is still administered where the kings, who were not only priests but lawyers, lived up as best they could to the wisdom of Solomon. The Parisian, tearing by in his taxi to see his lawyer, sets his watch by the first public clock ever set up in France, placed there before the fourteen hundreds had begun. It has been reconstructed, but it is still '*l'Horloge du Palais.*'

Just beside it is the round tower which had seen the agony of four centuries of prisoners before Marie Antoinette was brought there, to find what harmony she could in the broken chords of a life begun in imperial splendour, and ended in the public beastliness of a felon's death.

In the main courtyard of this Palace of Justice once stood the maypole, its ribbons only brighter than those of the lasses and lads who danced round it. The Sainte-Chapelle reared its jewel-rich windows beside the dancers. Later, shopmen displayed trinkets and lace and fine linen here, proud that the fine glasswork of their shops should make the courtyard one of the show places of Paris.

This courtyard is also one of the roadways of Paris. As, on legal business intent, one hurries across the uncoloured rectangle, where no maypole is remembered and no one ever dances, St. Louis' Chapel is still on the left; the business-like Law Courts are in front; on the right is a low archway, leading to the restaurant. Here congregate lawyers and clients, each with their hopes. Here, in 1918 and 1919, came the journalists of France and many countries, to write a hasty message for their papers, and snatch a hasty meal, between important testimonies upstairs, while Duval or Bolo was being tried for his life, in a room where a large blank panel testifies to the thoroughness with which atheistic France has removed even paintings of the Crucifixion from its halls of justice, lest perhaps justice be tempered with mercy. Here sat journalists and counsel. Here sat the people who were going to be allowed to use, for half an hour, a ticket enabling them to enter the place where one man was threatened with death for betraying his country – a sufficiently surprising spectacle to those who for over four years had braved death to save her; surprising also even to the civilian who, comfortable to a humiliating degree between his air-raids, when the roar of daily traffic had died down felt as if it were his own heart-beats the distant thud-thud of the guns along the front.

A curious assembly, and a curious restaurant; and a curious room. There, where we borrowed each other's fountain-pens, and swallowed scrambled eggs, and wondered if our message would get off in time for the country edition – there stood the tumbrils, waiting, as

23

neatly in rotation as omnibuses, and as indifferently, to be filled with passengers for the guillotine. The condemned came down the same little staircase that exists to-day, and, just about where our pepper castor stood, a proud foot mounted to the cart. When it was full, rumble-rumble out it went, under the archway which now bears the words 'Buffet-Restaurant,' over the Cour du Mai, and turned sharp to the left through the very bonnet of an unimagined motor-bus.

For centuries the pedestrian on his way to the North bank was compelled to cross movable planks, between which the mud oozed up as he walked, for the Pont Notre-Dame ended in a marsh long after its wooden piers had been replaced by stone. It was crowded with houses and shops, and saw one of the queerest roadside scenes when, in June, 1590, the ecclesiastical infantry of the Ligue was passed in review by the Papal Legate; 'Capucins, Moines, Cordeliers, Jacobins, Carmes, Feuillants, all with frock tucked up, hood lying back, helmet on head, shield on back, sword at side and musket on shoulder, walking four by four, the reverend Bishop of Senlis at their head, with a half-pike, and the curés of Saint-Jacques de la Boucherie and of Saint-Côme acting as Sergeant-majors.' Unfortunately, there was more enthusiasm than experience in the ranks of this church-militant. Wishing to salute the Legate, some of the volunteers, 'without thinking that their guns were loaded with ball,' shot a volley, and killed an almoner who was near the Pope's envoy. The envoy seems to have been a very tactful man, for, according to the Lazare brothers, he merely exclaimed, 'My friends, the June sun is too hot; it inconveniences me!' Then he gave them his blessing and 'went away'.

The only alternative means of reaching 'the town' (Paris to this day is divided into Town, City and University) was a little out of the traveller's way. The Pont au Change was already in existence west of the Pont Notre-Dame in Roman days, except, of course, when it had just been burned or flooded away, and had not yet been rebuilt in either stone or wood. Its double row of high houses was affected to the use of money-changers (to whom jewellers and goldsmiths were soon added) in 1141. A picturesque anecdote attributes their preference for this spot to the fact that the road from Jerusalem and

Rome, from Antwerp and Ghent and Canterbury and Winchester, here passed their doors, with all its traffic of simple-minded travellers, some with rich purses; while their back windows overhung the Seine – a useful situation if the King's officers came to test the coinage, when stores of false money meant for those travellers could be safely and rapidly disposed of out of these same windows.

Pleasanter folk were the bird-merchants, who were allowed to bring their songsters for sale to the bridge on holidays and Sundays, on condition that they would let loose two hundred dozen little birds there whenever kings or queens made their solemn entry to Notre-Dame. Bird-sellers are now every Sunday on the neighbouring market-place, and have permanent shops upon the adjacent Quai de la Mégisserie, called after the hide-workers.

Meanwhile, under the bridge, the butchers slaughtered their animals, and tanners carried on their unfragrant work. Sweet indeed must have smelled the pilgrims' gold in the nostrils of the usurers above to enable them to support such a neighbourhood!

In the sixteenth century there was a seller of unicorns' horns in her little shop on the bridge. These were very useful to travellers because they had the property of disliking impurities. Thus, if the horn of a unicorn touched anything poisoned, that horn sweated blood, although it was so hard that it could pierce the finest armour of Toledo. A time came when this was challenged; but the names of Brantôme and Ambroise Paré were little known till they had themselves adventured far into the Great Perhaps, and their opinions would have been to the earnest students tramping from university to university 'very advanced'; to the cheery Mistress Quickly of their wayside halts, a babbling; and to the friendly minds of the towns they passed, a something for which we have now been forced to invent the substantive, adjective, epithet, reproach, or garland – the disyllable 'highbrow.'

Ambroise Paré, great doctor and something of a sceptic, was doubtful about the unicorn. He had never seen one, and that was disconcerting. Of their horns he had seen plenty – the King's own specimen, three metres long, was in the Abbey of Saint-Denis; but he had put it to the test, and it did not sweat blood; and he therefore

25

categorically placed it among 'those of the Paris tradesmen, sold at high prices,' which were not true ones, 'because it is these I have tested.' Then he testifies to the honesty of a good lady on the Pont au Change who sold horns big and little, old and young, and always kept one in a vessel of water, and let everybody who liked drink of that water. This was no mean privilege, for at that time kings preserved themselves from poison by having a piece of unicorn's horn placed in their drink; and gold was 148 crowns a pound, while unicorn's horn was 1,536 crowns for the same weight.

Therefore it would be a bold pilgrim, an independent student indeed, who would go north or south across the bridges without drinking of this water or buying a small charm made of the unseen and unknown animal's horn. He was, of course, unless mentally deficient, already provided with a shark's tooth, which he firmly believed to be what the merchant had said it was – a serpent's tongue. 'Tis softer than a serpent's tooth to be a credulous child; but those credulities were as fruitful of war, quarrel, mental strife and self-conquest, as any dragon's teeth that ever were sown.

The traveller, then, with his crucifix in his breast, his bottle in his pocket, his belief in a personal devil rendering every shadow a danger, his dark experience of human nature making every drink an adventure, said his prayers at Notre-Dame, drank his unicorn water and broth, and stepped bravely northward.

Once upon the Northern bank, the traveller stopped at the inn of the Pomme de Pin, recommended by one Rabelais; and when he left it, if he could see them, he had before him the two roads which still spring unmistakably to the eye upon any map of Paris, or any map of northern France. For miles on either route he would be sped upon his way by monasteries, and as he went he would catch up with cheerful rotund friars, perhaps taking home their Thursday catch of fish from the Menilmontant, the pleasant little hill-stream gurgling its way down to the Seine, one of the lost rivers of Paris, as Tyburn is of London.

The Rue Saint-Martin of to-day is the natural continuation of the Rue Saint-Jacques. It follows it in the straight line beloved of the Romans; and it still turns off to the north-east and Flanders by

26

the Gare de l'Est and the church of Saint-Laurent, just where it did eighteen centuries ago. The Rue Saint-Denis is the road to the cliffs of Dover and the towers of Canterbury. But as soon as Paris had become an important civic centre, it took on a character of its own. There is nothing like it in London. Even in Paris, where the roads to the old Palaces are still distinct and clear, to Vincennes, to Versailles, to Fontainebleau, to Compiègne, the Rue Saint-Denis is unique.

No Frenchman anxious to be modern will admit that Saint Denis, having been decapitated on the slopes of Montmartre, took up his head and walked with it under his arm to a rather undistinguished spot where he thought it would be well to be buried. Yet the tradition was strong enough to produce an Abbey five miles north of Paris, and to make it the main symbol in the spectacle of French monarchy. The kings of France entered their capital from Saint-Denis, and when they had done their best, or worst, for their country, their tired bodies were carried along this same highway, with great pageantry that could dazzle them no more.

Upon the balconies and high window-sills of the Rue Saint-Denis the loyal bourgeoisie hung their best carpets and tapestries to embroider the passing of their sovereign. Outside their houses they put their dressers, main ornament of that sacred spot, the dining-room; all bedecked with every vessel of gold, silver, or pewter that could be mustered in honour of the royal wayfarer. Little wooden theatres were set up at intervals, where Mysteries were presented; bands played; fountains of scented waters flung themselves very usefully upon the crowd, and others ran with wine, hypocras and milk. Elaborate processions escorted the state entry. The Seven Virtues and the Seven Sins accompanied them as cheerfully as so many Jacks-in-the-Green; symbolic ceremonies halted their steps here and there. Isabelle of Bavaria (naughtiest of Queens in a Paris which had not yet met with Catherine of Medicis, or her daughter, Margot of Navarre) had been crowned with gold and jewels at the outer gates, by cupids creakingly lowered from a sham heaven, miles before she arrived at the Pont au Change, where a torch-bearer rather appropriately descended on a rope to wave flames about her.

27

All these monarchs stopped at the monastery, now the prison, of Saint-Lazare for a little while (hence the popular fury which pillaged the place in '92). There was a room called 'Le Logis du Roi,' and, alive or dead, the King tarried there for a space. A strange room it must have been, filled with the ghosts of hopeful youths elated by the thought that nothing was impossible for a ruler, and nothing too noble; of young brides dreaming of romance and weighted with dignities; of dead kings, all their hopes and disappointments, all their failures and their greatness, melted into the impassive wax of death. And like an invisible dado round the walls stood the ambitions and jealousies and ruthlessness harboured in the dark proud hearts of centuries of courtiers. There is something significant in the little fact that the nobles who accompanied the dead king to Saint-Denis were constrained to go afoot till the pause at Saint-Lazare was over; then, ready for a new king, for new intrigues, for new ambitions, they went a-horseback.

In that room, too, must surely have lingered the ghost of that same Isabelle of Bavaria, whose double coronation when she came as a bride to the city is recorded by Froissart; who had a second triumphal entry when she had married her daughter, 'la plus belle Katharine du monde,' to Henry V of England, and managed to be the most important figure in the conqueror's procession; and who, by private infamies which she was too corrupt to conceal, and by public treacheries, had surrounded herself with so much hatred that, when she reached death by the road of poverty and loneliness, her body had to be rowed hastily out of the city at night by a few hired men and shovelled, without honours, into the space left beside the bones of her mad husband. A dreadful ghost, even for that dreadful room, where the new kings must stay for a while, thinking of other things than death. Then they had to continue through the canyon of the Rue Saint-Denis to the waterside. There they must run the gauntlet of the tall houses on the bridge, where every window was weighted with faces, and an inconceivable soft tumult of wings beat upon the ears as two and a half thousand of little birds were restored to the use of the air.

When the monarchs went forth to be buried at Saint-Denis there were no wings, no fountains of hypocras or milk; the people crowding the wayside to watch the chanting monks and flickering candles had no better employment than to think what a great day it would be when the next king rode in.

The Rue Saint-Denis runs still through a Paris which has forgotten its old glories. Yet there is not a street in any European capital more constantly decorated, as if for the passage of Royalty. There is a fine pageantry upon its window-sills. This perpendicular line of scarlet is heraldic in its intensity; it is made by imitation leather hand-bags, and neither the scarlet nor the usefulness will last; but it makes a brave show. Here is a tapestry of colour: it is composed of cheap socks, four parasols, some bottles of highly-aniline perfume – efficiently corked, by the mercy of Heaven; carpet slippers which have some romantic aspirations to be as varied as stained glass; and long, snake-slim, coal-shiny belts, vermilion and cobalt and black and star-white, with a mouth and a fang of steel by which to buckle them. Near by hang splendid banners – gules and or and azure, gardens of woven and printed flowers, waving bravely in the air among the netted mazes of varicoloured string bags. These are the morning aprons and overalls of the local housewife.

On the upper floors, the old lane where Saint Denis went staggering to his tomb is caparisoned still. Here's a great drooping rectangle of fluffy cream-colour; the artist has drawn lines of sapphire and crimson across it. Here's a swift-falling torrent of white, with sharp blue shadows. Lolling over the two is a fat mass of indefinite paleness. The goodwife of Saint-Denis, who has no king living or dead, has hung out her blankets and sheets and bolsters to air.

The windows of the Rue Saint-Denis are not romantic, but they are never barren. They show bright scarves of artificial silk for sale where the first owners of those strange Oriental objects, carpets, displayed their possessions in honour of a monarch's passing; and the indifferent wind flaps the one, as it flapped the other, in the face of the busy passer-by.

Nowadays, whether one dwells at the gates of a palace or over a cheap leather shop, one must resort, if one wants to make the house look gay outside, to the standardized cheap bunting of commerce.

Nobody thinks their carpet a suitable decoration; it is either too ordinary or too precious. One buys a mixed lot of international flags, incorrectly printed, and hangs them on inferior string from the window-sill. At the first shower they become blended in a manner not yet achieved by Geneva. Times have changed; if you hung your brocade curtains over your balcony to welcome a passing monarch, you would simply be suspected of spring-cleaning.

It would be safe to conclude that of all the lovers of Paris who visit her from abroad scarcely one ever follows the Winchester road through Saint-Denis, nor the Saint-Denis road through Paris. It is not explored by even the most enterprising chars-à-banc. Yet this very ground, as definite as a bean-row or a furrow, was pressed by the tired bare feet of pilgrims; swept by the slow golden robes of kings' horses; traversed by the dull, deep step of men bearing in heavy coffins those whose pride had vanished into silence.

The tall houses hesitate in their straight sequence where merchants of fish had beaten a path round a hillock or a mud-patch so long before the Romans came that even they allowed the straight road of their preference to waver a little. The most magnificent of monarchs swept away the fortifications which had frowned at the cheerful approaching processions and gloomed behind the bier of dead majesty. The two triumphal arches of Louis XIV at the Portes Saint-Denis and Saint-Martin were henceforth to dazzle the eyes of thronging merchants on their mules, with a string of laden hacks or asses behind them; of envoys from great courts; of milords in their calèches. Henceforth Paris was to say, 'See how splendid and beautiful I am,' instead of 'See how formidable and strong I am.' The bulwarks had become the boulevards.

2: THE VERTEBRAE

THE NORTH-SOUTH ROADS OF PARIS FOLLOWED THE NEEDS OF THE miserable fisher-settlement which formed the nucleus of the brilliant Paris of yesterday and to-day. The river runs east to west, and it was not for centuries that the land-roads achieved the importance of the water-roads which had first made Lutetia a place worthy of attention. The Seine was the Bath Road of Paris till late in her history. It was only when patient engineering had worked for many generations that anybody travelled by land if he could travel by water.

The thoroughfare from Vincennes to Neuilly has therefore a different character from the roads that centre upon Notre-Dame. It bore no stream of pilgrims, and played little part in the plans of Imperial Rome. Its one likeness with the north-south highways is its thick hedge of monasteries, convents and churches, a hedge as inevitable upon a mediaeval town-road as are ferns in a Devonshire lane. It carried no special Parisian traffic, was identified with no trade. The Rue Saint-Jacques and the Rue Saint-Denis are charts of human endeavour, of the travail of human spirit, of the evanescent greatness of kings, whose splendour was once seen by the road-dwellers in a smiling figure upon a caparisoned charger, once in a long draped box borne by chanting monks, and then never more. The Rue Saint-Antoine and the Rue Saint-Honoré form the sun-path of human glory. They are double-lined with forlorn palaces, dismantled fortresses of grandeur, having that indescribable touch upon the heart of remembered sunsets and loved old ladies.

One could walk upon a definite highway north and south through Paris, but to go from east to west was not so easy. The old Roman road from Melun, later dedicated to Saint Antoine, had to go round the Bastille; Saint Honoré's had to avoid the convent and cemetery of the Innocents, for church property was respected even after a king's head had fallen. So to this day the follower of the old road must pass through the Rue de la Ferronnerie. Henry IV had to do so in order to visit Sully, who was lying ill in an over-sculptured palace just behind that Place Royale (or des Vosges), which the two

31

had planned and built together in the days when Jean Goujon could make symbolic figures, and younger men were trying to, as may be seen in the courtyards of the Hôtels Carnavalet and Sully.

Henry IV was the most illustrious example of the evil that lies in procrastination. He lived in enlightened days – one was not the slave of superstition in these late times, when the sixteenth century was already dead. Notions of town-planning were rife, and there was no convent or monastery in the street of the iron-workers and cart-makers to prevent one tearing down one side of it and making it commodious and ample. But the project remained one – there were other things to think of; hence the carriage of the King, who was reading state papers, had to slow down so much, owing to the obstruction of new and old carts, that Ravaillac could approach the cheerful man and plunge a stolen carving-knife into his body.

Not until Napoleon served his glory by opening the Rue de Rivoli could the east and west of Paris see each other. Then the ruins of the Bastille looked at the unfinished Arc de Triomphe; and till the first were cleared away and the second was finished, the life of the little Corsican did straddle Paris as Caesar straddled Rome.

Entering Paris from the east, one is escorted by thoughts of the unmoved grey donjon of Vincennes behind; that tower which was the country-house of Saint Louis, saw the long martyrdom of the Man in the Iron Mask and the death of Henry V of England, and presided with the same stone countenance over the deaths of the shabby little men who tried to sell France for money when she was buying herself with blood between 1914 and 1918. There is not much of a gate at this entrance to Paris; but this was the road on which walked the volunteers from Marseilles who came into Paris singing the 'Tipperary' of the day, called after them the 'Marseillaise,' although it was written by a youngster of the Jura when he was in Strasbourg. They passed over the place where the guillotine was to be erected, troubling as little about the falling of blood as anglers trouble about the personal sufferings and domestic bereavements of the fish they catch.

On this same Place de la Nation is held the annual gingerbread fair. There you can ride on gilded horses, or in large plaster wash-

"*Double-lined with forlorn palaces*"

basins, while the hurdy-gurdy plays beneath, on the very spot where heads fell into a basket; one can buy singularly sticky nougat just where some bored employees of the town lugged your trunk and legs away to the town dust-cart, sweating a bit, and planning to ask more wages to-morrow for a hot job like this.

They walked on through the Revolution's own street, of Saint Antoine, 'the finder of lost things,' to the Bastille, sexton of lost men. The Bastille has fallen. There is not a resident of Paris who does not regret it on every fourteenth of July, except those young enough to dance all night, to the music of orchestras that make their elders lie awake cursing Liberty, Fraternity and Equality. A thousand trams concentrate with screaming brakes where the prisoners of the Bastille lay in silence and darkness. Life swirls over the spot as water swirls over a wreck.

Here begins a line of palaces three miles long. Many of them are still visible, though the needs of commerce are rapidly diminishing their number. Royalty, like religion in old days and dressmaking in these, moved west. The Palace of Saint Paul succeeded the Palace of the Tournelles and preceded the Louvre; the Tuileries came next; and by this time progress in the amenities of life, as typified by its road-making, had reached such a pitch that people could go to Saint-Germain or Versailles for three o'clock dinner and be back again the same night. Hence the two long lines of stately mansions which constitute the Faubourgs Saint-Germain and Saint-Honoré. The Court followed the King, always westward, leaving behind it the older mansions, nowadays submerged by the tide of wholesale trade as the buried cities of the south coast have been submerged by the waters of the Channel, leaving only ghostly bells ringing in the ears of the Devon and Cornwall men. Here and there an island has survived, such as the Place des Vosges, the Hôtel Carnavalet, or the Archives, whose courtyard is a very pretty piece of paving, and ought by rights to be red instead of grey, if blood were indelible, for there was plenty spilt in the days when the de Rohans and the de Guises kept house there as majestically, as despotically, and as passionately as kings.

Another island is the Place de Grève; that open space before the Hôtel de Ville whose name, by the incidence of history upon language, has come to mean in all men's minds something like downing tools, or something like being executed, rather than something like a sloping river bank. A little frightened by these dark associations of the past, and darker commentaries on the future, the municipal authorities have godfathered the Place de Grève into the Place de l'Hôtel de Ville. This is only another form of that simplified spelling which is designed to make a royal road to learning for those who are too lazy to learn, and to turn a penniless word wi' a lang pedigree into a useful one with no pedigree at all.

In the sixteenth century the Place de Grève was a centre of activity — as activity was understood in the days before the word 'hustle' had been sent back across the Atlantic in reprisal for the endeavour of Christopher Columbus. But it took its holidays. In order to amuse folk who had a day off on St. John's Eve, it burned cats alive for the public pleasure; thus getting well ahead of Salem, which burned cat-owners as witches. They were hung from a high tree in a basket or barrel, or even a sack, to the number of a couple of dozen or so, and the tree was set alight. The royal trumpets and musicians left off playing, so that no sound might be lost. On one occasion a fox was added to the screaming victims, because it was thought that the King and the Royal Family, who always attended the festival, would like this. A fortnight later Charles IX gave the signal for a fête on a larger scale, but not of a very different nature, and stood at a window of the Louvre, listening to the cries of the victims of St. Bartholomew's Eve.

It was a hundred years after Wolsey had offended Henry VIII by Hampton Court and Somerset House that another Cardinal built himself a Palais-Cardinal. Richelieu chose a spot opposite the Louvre and next door to the mushroom Tuileries. He installed himself close at hand, and had a house only less grand, a garden only less large, than the King's. In all his thinking, did he ever imagine that such a man as Camille Desmoulins would ever exist; would ever have a statue put up to him; or that his own cherished garden would become a thoroughfare for the public, and that statue, of all statues, be set in that place, of all places, for admiration?

The Palais Royal to-day is a dead garden, filled with footsteps of busy people who do not stop even to look at its splendid Rodin, and the patterings of children who cannot play hide-and-seek round it, because in Republican France all must keep to the gravel-walks of the people's gardens. Richelieu's home has fallen from its magnificence to the utility of a public pathway, through a long history of debauch and sordid nastiness.

Richelieu wanted a home for his grandeur; Mazarin wanted a home for his books. His palace has known some strange moments. He made a library, not only for himself, but for all book-lovers – the first public library (a conception of Richelieu, by the way). Then kings and queens used it as their home. Then the wildest frenzy of speculation took it. John Law was to Paris what the South Sea Bubble was to London. He was housed in Mazarin's great dwelling, and none can paint the fever of the would-be rich and the ruined who paced this courtyard; some hurrying to fling to the Golden Calf their farm in Normandy, their small daughter's dowry; others stepping slowly and heavily away to tell their wives that henceforward the family is homeless and penniless. From this, by some native attraction exercised by books, the Palais Mazarin returned again to its use as a bookhouse; its happy destiny to be filled by bookworms. It is now the Bibliothèque Nationale, and smells of half-calf instead of golden calf.

If there are islands in the westward current, there are also whirlpools. The largest is the white space of the Place de la Concorde, with trees kept back from it behind balustrades on two sides, like crowds at a football match, and some august buildings looking at each other from north and south. The river runs by between these buildings, but it might be subterranean for all one can see of it; it is only represented above-ground by two slanting parapets and the characteristic upward road of a bridge. At night the Place is set about with so many lights that it looks like Queen Elizabeth's diamond stomacher. When in war-time the lighting was diminished almost to vanishing point, the great square under the moon, with its silent obelisk and stilled fountains, had a dream-like beauty which it never has in normal times. Vast even under the blaze of a summer sun, it then looked as spacious as some silver desert in a fairy-tale, with the glowing eyes of monsters moving about it as the rare taxis passed. Efficient municipal lighting has robbed it of its mystery, and no one who looks at it on a fine afternoon can deny its physical likeness to a busy eddy in a swift river; but its symbolic resemblance to the Maelstrom is of a darker nature.

On a stone in the corner house which used to be the palace of the Crillons, and now is the chosen hotel of political bigwigs, there is still to be read the inscription 'Place Louis XVI.' This reminder of the first victim of the Terror was one of the tributes paid to the old *régime* at the time of the Restoration. It remains sedately upon the wall, as a good street-name should, a little defaced by time and out-shone by the neighbouring words, 'Place de la Concorde,' but still bearing witness to the fact that for ten years the penultimate Louis was honoured by the last Louis.

The names borne by this open space, which has been likened to the Great Square of Ispahan, have been: Louis XV, Revolution, Concorde, Louis XVI, and Concorde. The name of Concord was invoked when the guillotine was removed. Legend tells that a nest of doves was found in the globe upheld by the statue of Liberty that once stood there ; it was time that a dove or an olive-branch visited this place. It is recorded that when the guillotine was still there a herd of cattle fled bellowing and snorting because their drovers wished to lead them across it; but the smell of blood was insupportable – to them.

Among the gay and careless doings of young Marie Antoinette, the lovely, petted, high-spirited creature, was a winter drive with the Princesse de Lamballe. Down the Champs Elysées they came, in a golden sleigh with jingling golden bells, wrapped in furs, laughter in their eyes and their voices. They were to themselves two girls running gleefully loose for an hour or two from eternal etiquette, eternal courtiers, eternal ladies-in-waiting. No pair of schoolgirls could have more enjoyed the escapade. Here was a fine outing, with restraints and disapproval left well behind at Versailles, and Paris glittering in the snow before them! The sleigh ran smoothly, there was no taint in the air to repel the horses, and the light-hearted queen was drawn without a shudder over the spot where in a few years the drums rolled as her husband's head fell into the basket; and across

36

the square to the place where the guillotine was to claim her also. At the most she may have told the coachman to drive quickly, because she hated to remember that in the deep ditches round the square more than a thousand people were trampled to death during her wedding fête.

Both her friends and her enemies have recorded that Marie Antoinette, the white-haired old woman of thirty-seven, never flinched upon her tumbril-road along the Rue Saint-Honoré, never heeded insult or stone; but did turn a whiter cheek towards the Tuileries when she found that for her the guillotine had been set up as near as possible to the green garden where her little son had played. Taxis roll over the spot now, past the Strasbourg statue, and if there is a block, every accent from Hammerfest to 'Frisco and back to Moscow exclaims that traffic should be better managed. Yet it needs all the municipal lighting, and more, to keep the Place de la Concorde free of ghosts.

There is at any rate one matter-of-fact Frenchman who will never forget a vision he had there one night. In 1917 a Scottish general sent half a dozen pipers to Paris for the St. Andrew's Night dinner of the Scottish community. There was to eat, there was to drink, there was that acutest form of homesickness which visits exiles in war-time; and the music of the pipes skirled and whirled till none could count the R's in the skirling and the whirling. At an hour so very late that it was no longer even very early, one piper was missed. A search-party issued forth into the still November night, or rather, the still December morning, and finally they found him.

He was striding round the northern fountain in the Place de la Concorde, calling the Clans to battle. Claymores flashed in every note, the battle-axes of the chieftains were in the reed; his kilt swung, his undaunted knees carried him sturdily, his distended cheeks held the unbroken pibroch; and the terrifying eye of a Highlander in his pride surmounted all. All around him spread the huge spaces of the moon-white square; and in one corner, lit sparely by a war-time lamp, the seekers beheld the diminishing figure of a Paris policeman (usually the most redoubtable of beings), cape flapping, baton dropped, fleeing for sanctuary at police headquarters from this visible and far too audible visitant of the night. There is no evidence that he had informed himself as to whether the resounding ghost was also tangible.

The Champs Elysées, a tree-garden interspersed with unexpected theatres, and illuminated with stone-walled ponds which cry aloud for lily-leaves and reflected Tudor walls, and have to be content with modern sculptured fountains – the Champs Elysées also include the two main exhibition halls of Paris. The Grand Palais has a catholic spirit; it houses paintings and horses and motor-cars and aeroplanes. Once, in that odd pre- or inter-historic time known as 'during the war' it had wounded men there. It is very Large, and it is very Handsome. Over the way the Petit Palais hugs itself to itself. It has no vulgarities, and very seldom advertises its exhibits; and in its heart is a little garden where water plashes lazily, and flowers smell sweetly, and the distant noise of traffic might be the voice of Seville or Verona.

In the Avenue des Champs Elysées (usually confounded by visitors with the Champs Elysées themselves) one can see what Long Acre might make of itself if it had Park Lane to play with. The luxurious motor-car has captured many a ground floor here; dressmaking, with a capital D in a woman's mouth, and nine in the mouth of her husband, is firmly installed upstairs. There is hardly a spot in Europe where something you don't really need can be bought at a higher price than in the Avenue des Champs Elysées. It is also breaking out into theatres and restaurants, which all start off on top super-prices, but lower their notes later. Even in this avenue de luxe there are limits to the spending capacity of its frequenters.

The Travellers' Club was La Pavia's house, and still encloses her silver bath. Every one who is Anyone belongs to this club. It was also very useful to the general public during the war as a spot where one could get an evening taxi in the times of shortage; and it would be difficult to have found then, or to find now, a more fruitful source of stories concerning the kind of bridge which deserves a European reputation.

The Rue and the Faubourg Saint-Honoré have preserved many of their stately buildings, and have much more dignity, if less beauty, than the Rue de Rivoli and the Champs Elysées behind them. But one cannot break eggs without having something like an omelette; and all the old splendours of lovely women with shining shoulders and gleaming jewels, and talented and witty men, are now more easily to be found in the Embassy Wellington bought for England, or the Inter-Allied Club beloved of Americans, than in the President's palace next door.

There is an omnibus which runs along this route. It starts from the district where the fourteenth-century nobles built their houses to be near the King; it carries its passengers through the cheapest shopping district of Paris, where one buys onions and bread, to the dearest, where one buys silk stockings and silly little hand-bags and flimsy ultra-modern furniture. Incidentally, it passes the spot where pig-merchants were allowed to let their herds run loose among the rubbish of the town; where men were hanged in chains and left to rot; where Joan of Arc was wounded; and where Napoleon dislodged with cannon-balls the rebels who had taken refuge in the Church of Saint-Roch. The conductor, passing over the site of the old Saint-Honoré gate, round which these things happened, will merely state that it is a '*changement de section*,' and ask for more money.

Either by the old road of the Faubourg Saint-Honoré, which very naturally skirted the hill, or by the ruler-straight Champs Elysées, upon whose apex Napoleon equally naturally placed his Arc de Triomphe, one arrives at the Place de l'Etoile, the crowning glory of Haussmann's work for Paris. From a junction of roads at one of the barriers, dignified only by the Arc de Triomphe, he evolved the present twelve-pointed star, which is now the most lively death-trap for the pedestrian. Even soldiers and sailors have been known to lose their nerve half-way across the swirling road, and stand with closed eyes helplessly waiting to know what will knock them down first. There are no protected crossings here as in the Avenue des Champs Elysées; and this is strange, because, since the Unknown Soldier was buried under the Arch, there are few Parisians and no tourists who do not wish to walk past his grave.

The most impressive time to wait on him is about 2 a.m. It is dark under the Arch, but stars look in high up, and the lights of Paris lying below make a ring about him. Every footstep sounds loudly at that hour; the slow pace of the policeman, the hurried patter of belated citizens, the firm gait of the occasional visitor who has come across the road in order to pass this spot, make a kind of weaving-air, to which the bourdon of the distant traffic is an accompaniment. The slope of the ground is accentuated by the darkness, and when one looks up into the dark mass overhead one seems to be in a cellar; but when one looks outward it is like standing on a hill remote from noise and littleness, keeping guard in august company over something much greater than a great city.

The proportions of the Arch are very misleading. The enormous height of it diminishes the apparent width of the central opening; but an aeroplane has before now flown through it at full speed. From the sides, the Arch is really hideous; nothing but turning it upside down could make sightly the narrow opening with its unspeakably heavy top-hamper. The depth of it is less than half its width, much less than half its height. The side arches are only one-sixth of the height. Seen from the Avenue Carnot, or the Avenue Victor-Hugo, it is an enormity. One cannot be too thankful that its magnificent fronts, its deformed sides, have not been diminished or accentuated by the typically Louis-Philippean idea of surrounding it with 'statues of illustrious soldiers of the empire and the republic'!

On the extreme western limit of Paris stood until recently the Chateau de la Muette. It is still remembered in a street-name; but vanished is the royal country-house where the shy child Marie Antoinette held her first reception in France, and where her red-faced brother-in-law, as hearty as a tapster and as malicious as a schoolboy, stood to watch with glee the Return from Versailles. His daughter and his elder son (the boy was sixteen years old that day) stood by him, smiling when he smiled, as loved children will do before life has taught them the bitter lesson that perhaps the opinions of Father himself must be questioned. La Muette is well away; it was a place where ghosts wring their hands, and old ribbons and old portraits are consigned to a dust that falls thick but does not obliterate.

On the Left Bank, the University was left to itself for centuries, and had no use for thoroughfares going west. When the great folk

VAL DE GRACE

came across the river to make a kind of Peacehaven of their own, they built along cow-tracks and cart-ruts – hence the Rues Saint-Dominique, de Varenne, de Grenelle – and used the old roads of Cherche-Midi and Vaugirard.

The usual hedge of monasteries and hospitals soon began to grow beside it. They have mostly been swept away, but the Hôpital Laënnec still remains. It was once the *Incurables*, but long after his death the young doctor who invented the stethoscope was given a coldly civil thank-you by his country, when it clamped his name on to a hospital which should have borne the names of its founders.

On this same road remained until a few years before the Abbaye aux Bois. It stood in the street 'of Sèvres' that was once the highway of noble France from its Faubourg Saint-Germain to its pleasaunce at Versailles. But to-day, if one mentions the name, the invariable reply, whether in English, French, German or American, is: 'Oh yes; where the Bon Marché is!' The Abbaye stood in the Saint-Germain quarter, where stately houses stand back in odd corners, their only sign the massive doors that give on to some narrow side street. The students' quarter has encroached on the ancient Faubourg from one side, while the irresistible tide of commerce pours through it from the other. The great hotels that remain, with splendid names carven over their doors, such as 'De la Rochefou-cauld-Doudeauville,' or historic arms done in time-worn stone, are like so many sand-castles turned to islands by the rising tide, and one by one they crumble and vanish. What ancient splendour could resist a tidal wave that bore upon its crest the words 'Bon Marché'?

The three-sided buildings of the Abbaye aux Bois fronted on the Rue de Sèvres from 1640. In 1654 it was sold to the Sisters of the Order of Citeaux, whose ancient Abbaye aux Bois, in Noyon, was become uninhabitable by reason of the civil wars and pillage which Anne of Austria's regency let loose upon the land. They brought the name of their Abbaye with them and, in their new quarters, flourished very much. Their convent school became the best known in Paris after the Sacré Cœur, and the buildings grew until the original Abbaye was tripled in size. Then the frontage to the Rue de Sèvres was placed at the disposal of ladies who wished to go

41

into semi-retirement. The chief of them was the beautiful Madame Récamier.

For nearly thirty years she lived here, and the Abbaye became the first literary resort in France. In the small, bare rooms with their whitewashed walls, heavy oak beams, and red-tiled floors, Chateaubriand's *Mémoires d'Outre-Tombe* were first read. In its last years the glory had departed from the old courtyard behind the iron gates that withstood the violence of the Revolution. On the cobbles over which Chateaubriand and Ballanche paced up and down, waiting for the doctor to bring them news of their beautiful friend, long after youth had left her, and afraid to ring lest she should know they were anxious, were spread out every few days hundreds of sponges, from a little shop over the way, laid in the sun to dry, and giving out a sharp, glorious sea-smell to the keen air. An old woman occasionally came to remake the mattresses of the *locataires*. She combed the wool between two boards set with spikes; unstitched, beat, cleaned, and remade as many as three mattresses a day on her wooden frame. Two or three babies learning to walk were perfectly safe behind the closed gates, for no carriage ever drove up.

Even this remnant of the life that once centred here soon went; already in 1907 the school had been dismissed, the school buildings and cloisters had been pulled down, and a few dusty shrubs and mutilated walks were all that were left of the convent garden. All but twenty-two of the very aged Sisters had been dismissed by the Government, whose will it was that the religious schools and Orders should be abolished. It was pathetic to see the nuns who remained, wandering in their garden at dusk, when the workmen had gone, watering tenderly what flowers remained during their last weeks of occupancy. There was, in one *appartement* in the Abbaye, an oratory with a grille overlooking the altar of the chapel, before which a single lamp was always burning. At vesper time there came from behind a carved wooden screen at one side of the altar the sound of low chanting, sometimes varied by sweet, high singing. All in the chapel was dark, save the one light before the altar. It was the nuns at evensong; but it would be easy to imagine that the crowding, brilliant ghosts of those who haunted the Abbaye for so many years were gathered in its doomed chapel to sing its requiem. And now a cinema and a block of flats occupy that sad old plot of ground.

Among nearly all these streets are house-high gates that remain closed to the world. Behind them dwell old gate-keepers, who slip in and out through half-doors to buy their bread and wine, and are so used to airing unused apartments and dusting ancient gildings that they would be horrified to see a coach, let alone a motor-car, drive into the courtyard. These are the houses of the remnant of the *ancien régime*, which left Paris when Paris rejected the Bourbons, and has lived in the provinces ever since on less and less money and more and more pride. In 1914 their sons went forth to fight for France – not for the Republic. Others of these houses are still the family homes; but all alike turn a blank face upon the passer-by, for what have they to do with him? They are too proud to know they are proud; too old to know they are bored; and so sure of themselves that to this day they are a city in themselves, untouched by Paris, and unwilling to touch it even with their own magnificent steel and bronze tongs.

The Rues Saint-Jacques, Saint-Martin and Saint-Denis are the spine of Paris; the Rues Saint-Antoine and Saint-Honoré and the Saint-Germain streets are its vertebrae. The underground and overground transports run every day along and between them; on every hand are scores of thoroughfares that have grown round them, and every one is rich in association. Abelard might have come running out of this door to decide whether you or your taxi-man had the better right to the disputed sum; Ruggieri could have cast a spell upon you for sniffing as you walked past that evil-smelling wall; a hundred couples shrink further under the trees as you pace this public walk – grocers and sewing-maids now, but monarchs and courtiers once. Paris is built upon few roadways, and not even her almond-shaped boulevards matter so much to her as these ancient tracks.

The boulevards between the Madeleine and the Rue Richelieu are the best-known streets in Paris; just as the March is the most celebrated 'morceau' of 'Faust,' and Miss Wilcox is celebrated for

'Laugh, and the World laughs with you.' But, like many over-tasted morsels, they have lost their flavour. Books have been written about them, and another one might be written yet; Louis XIV – D'Orsay – Queen Victoria; Dumas – Scribe – Bataille; Tortoni – Paillard – Café Napolitain; Monte-Cristo – Arthur Meyer – Ernest Daudet. But the boulevards are gone; nobody walks upon them to see and be seen (Lord Bertie was the last, parading in pearl-grey during the latest days of peace, in 1914); nobody goes there to eat beautifully instead of to feed with economy; duels are no longer arranged there; banks have replaced restaurants; the kinema has placed its proletarian foot where Horace Vernet's tie proclaimed that even an artist might also be a man of fashion; and as for anybody who buys anything in the average boulevard emporium, he pro-claims himself such a foreigner as was expected by such a shop. Scented gentlemen take made-up ladies to buy false pearls on the very spot where once keen-eyed archers looked northward over the marshes for crawling enemies, and men ran with lighted torches to set off the cumbrous cannon. And now even the trees are dying; petrol is killing them.

There are strange scraps of interest about the streets of Paris for those who care to look for them. For instance, there is a thoroughly matter-of-fact roadway near the Halles which is drearier than the Edgware Road and not so important; it is called the Rue Mondé-tour. It has been there for over six centuries. Here was the first well in which anybody drowned herself for love. Three centuries later a desperate lover tried to do the same thing; but he was un-romantically fished out and, even more unromantically, married his girl. He handsomely rebuilt the well, and it may be hoped that he did something for the local filters. Now clanging trams make thunder sounds across this spot.

Not far off, where those who know can find it, is a half-obliter-ated sculptured basin in a wall. Once a green-shaded fountain, it is very, very old, very, very worn; but Heloise and Abelard met there in the evening, as Bert and Gleddis do at the Piccadilly Tube Station; and it isn't their fault if the chap from Stratford is not there to dub them Romeo and Juliet.

Among the other strange oddments of the Paris streets is the uninteresting Rue Pierre Levée. Unlike many other French Peter streets, this one is not named after any notable chemist or politician or municipal functionary. The Pierre or Peter referred to is an upraised stone, the Pierre Levée of the Druids, because a menhir was found on this spot when it was levelled up in 1782. And who can tell what the Druids thought of the Revolution that flowed past their altar a few years after?

In one Paris street there is the only church dedicated to Saint Eugène; thus named by an infatuated emperor in honour of his wife. The interior is entirely made of cast-iron, and what the moral may be, God knows. It is certainly the least-known church of Paris.

In the Place des Abbesses there is a red-brick church which has inlays of blue and white tiles, very fussily disposed. Nobody can explain this either.

It is only the old streets which explain themselves; and it is true that, in spite of modern requirements, there are few modern buildings on the duffle-roads or the brocade-roads of Paris.

EVERY TRAVELLER IS MET AT THE STATION OR THE PORT OF EVERY foreign town by an impressive ambassador of its strangeness — the look of its streets. Tired with travel, harassed by porters and Customs officials, humiliated by the clack of an unknown or half-known tongue, and confused by a coinage which is apparently all give and no take, the adventurer into foreign lands still has a consciousness of streets beyond. It is probably dawn or dusk, and often rainy, these daunting attributes of arrival having been apparently plotted together by the railway staff and the bogies of twilight; the immediate foreground is occupied by a taxi with a cold-eyed and greedy god upon the box; the entire middle distance is trunks and porters; and an orchestra of voices, a frieze of outheld hands, surrounds all. But in the background are streets, looking different from known ones at home; an air that smells different; sounds that are foreign to experience; something new, so new that its novelty penetrates even the bother of arrival.

This impression deadens with familiarity. The impressive ambassador becomes the constant companion of every expedition and every walk; an interesting creature still, but no longer as awful and as enticing as a wizard, one goes arm-in-arm with him now. And when one goes away, he follows as humbly and as faithfully as a terrier to the station doors or the dock gates, and is so quickly forgotten that the returned traveller, only too prolix in regard to almost everything else, has no sense of carelessness in devoting a casual half-sentence to 'the foreign look of the streets,' although he might as well describe a portrait without describing the appearance of the sitter.

Paris is an astonishingly foreign city to London eyes, considering how near she is. She has so much that London lacks, and wants so much that the Londoner likes — although her physical beauty is so great that he is seldom aware of any defect till he has fallen out of love with her a little, and still less seldom analyses the reason for her 'foreign' look.

It resides principally, of course, in the Continental system of having flats over shops. This accounts for the uniformity of stucco frontages, and the presence of food-stores, restaurants, and cafés or wineshops in what would be strictly business quarters in an English city. There is only one district of Paris where almost all floors of almost all houses are used for commerce – the neighbourhood where the dingy streets are called after Napoleon's splendiose victories in Egypt. Even there, the top floors are dwelling-places. The main boulevards, apart from their side-streets, are nearly all offices, but a burst of flowers at a sixth- or seventh-floor window shows that a home is there. The ornately sterile face of the Steel Age has not yet entirely wiped from the Boulevard Montmartre or the Rue d'Abou-kir the quiet monotonous features of houses that, like trees, were built for people who, like birds, grubbed for a livelihood on the earth level, and whose nesting, living and breeding were done over-head in the tall bright air.

Paris shares with many another town of occidental Europe the stark shimmer of sunlit stucco. The western sun is refracted into eastern rooms from these unchanging faces with a Saharan piti-lessness during a heat-wave. Most streets in Paris, except in the very modern quarters where high commerce or foreign wealth are catered for (and drained), are narrow. A sou'westerly gale that slams the western windows will blow back again from eastern neigh-bours with noise of shattered glass, bringing strange broken calls of vessels that are only tugs upon the Seine, but might be, from their sonority, great ships going to breast great seas. The baked sunsets come back likewise, fighting the sun's own entry into the house, and one wonders at last if the uplifting green frontages of hostile waters are as terrifying as the oven-fronts of Paris streets in those heat-waves which take all courage from one, a thing not done to seamen by any sea.

The roofs of Paris are unexpected. They go up into series of windows caught like flies into nothing nearer to amber than is slate; they slope back or upwards into unlikely eminences; they are hard enough to be suspected of fossilizing their in-dwellers; yet in and out from their one or two, or even three, storeys move the most healthy and ardent humans – Monsieur Durand going to business, his wife going to market, his father wheeling his little son, his mother coming to a family dinner, and his sister-in-law and brother strolling

48

along in good time for the famous soup, and talking of little Jacques with many a thought of their own coming little Jean – who will be spoken of as openly and as heartily as young Jacques there present. These attic windows glow, through their shut panes, with the same family ardour that lights the first floor, where in the instant between lighting-up and closing the shutters one can see gilt ceilings and walls, and the bandy-legged brilliance of real or false Louis XV furniture.

There are red-tiled roofs here and there on Paris houses which have little to do with the super-modern face of the lower floors; and in the Champs Elysées themselves, from a third-floor window of that Travellers' Club where play runs high and a courtesan's silver bath is still preserved, the eye can range across the purring traffic of the wealth of five continents, up the sternly rapacious modern fronts of dressmaking houses where a yard of muslin costs a thousand francs, to old roofs studded with emerald moss. There is even one eighteenth-century roof in this thoroughfare; a gracious slating that has outlived that of Grosvenor House, though an hotel or a super-drapery store will soon have submerged the Duc de Massa's house. Nobody looks at it, nobody stops there (except one line of omnibuses), and its two-storied grace and deserted garden are like a breath from some dead fairy-tale. No one will ever tread its corridors again in high red heels and rustling silk and gem-bright towering hair; this is the oldest and most forgotten face that peers upon hooting new Paris, and before another winter it will have vanished.

The Mansard school has left its mark upon the roofs of Paris. Very few modern houses have the steep-sloped slating of the Hôtel de Mayenne; but one can still see in the upper floors of the Paris streets the Mansard pitch, as it has been modified into slants, windows and upright storeys by the increasing need for utilizing every inch of space. There are many buildings where wide balconies were arranged for in old days on the fifth floor, at the expense of smaller rooms, and which yet bear superimposed flats of garret-dwellings inserted by masons' surgery into the roof, and each putting forth a square-browed eye of window.

Most of the houses in Paris streets have balconies. Nowadays they have factory-made balustrades, but they used to have railings of tied iron, as lovely as that back staircase rail in the Hôtel de Beauvais, which is flaking away like cheese for want of painting. There is a front balcony in that same great old house, now let out in tenements – a balcony deprived of its beautiful iron fence, a balcony which reminds one of another in the Canongate. On that, Argyle and Murray watched Montrose, clad in scarlet and proud of eye, draw upwards to his death; on this, Anne of Austria and Mazarin watched Louis XIV and his bride pass towards their palace of the Louvre.

To this day, a lovely balcony of old times offers itself to the eye. It was built for a duke's private pleasure, as a remote country pavilion, and has become a silversmith's shop in the busiest and most tormented corner of Paris. The Pavillon de Hanovre, at the corner of the Rue Louis le Grand and the Boulevard des Capucines, in spite of advertisements about it and the winking of illuminated signs above, still presents the beautifully-made balustrade to which lovely ladies and gallant gentlemen stepped out from the candle-lit rooms to breathe the tree-cool air of the deserted fortifications; to whisper something quickly said but not easily forgotten; and perhaps to ponder upon the nightingale's busyness in this spot erstwhile dedicated to the tramp of sentinels and the roar of aroused guardsmen. Twenty dozen nightingales, orchestrated by Stravinsky and conducted by Honegger, could not be heard there now.

In these foreign-looking streets, as the eye comes down from roofs to balconies, past the tall, slatted outside shutters, one thing will strike everybody who is trying to understand the difference between the cosy dim streets of home and these canyons of glaring brightness. The numbers of the houses are placed so high that, unless the street is so wide that you cannot see across it, you cannot find the number at all without laying your head between your shoulder-blades. In wet weathers chauffeurs of taxis do wonders of camel-neckedness by peering under their canopies to the high first floors, where small blue plaques are affixed, with very large, thick numbers on them in white, so thick that 31 and 81, to a cricked neck, are difficult to distinguish. This is so much the case that the authorities have just invented a grand new scheme by which the number of the nearest house is to be pasted on the nearest lamp-post in cut-out black paper. It has not

"These foreign-looking streets"

occurred to anybody to ordain that each proprietor should put his number within eye-reach.

It is so usual for us to be identified like convicts or policemen in our streets or in our telephones that it is difficult to understand that the numbering of the Paris streets was once a matter of civic warfare. The owners of courtyards would have nothing of this encroachment on their liberties, and fought so strenuously against what seemed to them a degrading concession to democracy, that in fact it was only after the fall of the Bastille that these proud gateways were forced to bear a figure on their brows. There are traces of her wild history to be read even on the smugly uniform faces of the streets of Paris — even in the respectable blue enamel plaques which number her houses.

This is even more true of the neat blue and white parallelograms which tell the street-name. Glanced at by pedestrian and chauffeur, they are taken as matters of course by both, who use them and go carelessly on their way; but stern faces and hard struggles, high ambition and mean intrigue, are the ingredients which municipal alchemy has resolved into signs as bland and comfortable as a Sunday afternoon nap.

Numbers have almost banished the signs of other days. A few remain, such as the 'Gagne-Petit' in the Rue des Nonnains d'Hyères (the shop of that name has a copy in the Avenue de l'Opèra); but their usefulness vanished with the numbering of the houses, and with them went a thousand anecdotes, a thousand sidelights on history, a thousand reminders of the comedy and tragedy of human life. The modern renaissance of wrought-iron in France has given Paris some exquisite signs, but they are purely decorative. The days are gone when a man's house could only be found, his trade known, his name guessed, by the sign he hung out. Gone, too, the days when the fashionable feeling or craze was thus traced outside the houses, so that the Revolution made everything Bastille or Liberty; a theatrical craze produced shops called after popular plays; or a wave of punning told the literate world that behind the sign 0.20.100.0 one drank wine weakened by no water (*au vin sans eau*), and that a huge *I* in green (*au grand Hiver*) indicated that here one could buy enough logs to hearten the coldest day.

It may be a shock to romantics to find that the many French inns dedicated to *le Lion d'Or* celebrate no proud Knight with the Golden Lion on his shield, but only the fact that *au lit on dort*!

Once the tradesmen of Paris had made their signs so large and heavy that they were fined, and preferred to pay the fines rather than abandon 'leurs chères enseignes.' Now, if prosperous enough, they buy finely wrought signs which they hang out as beautifully – and as uselessly – as ear-rings.

Paris streets were organized before Paris houses were numbered. One lived on 'The Cow-Track in Little Montrouge,' for instance, or in 'the street by which one enters and leaves the quay and the garden of the Hôtel Saint-Denis'; and if the yet unnumbered house bore a sign, that was not only a means of receiving letters, but sometimes a useful name to take. Ducerceau, the architect of the Pont Neuf and the Hôtel Sully, was the son of a wineshop-keeper called Androuet, who, in accordance with police regulations, had to hang out a sign indicating the nature of his trade. He chose a barrel-hoop, and his son took it for his surname, and always signed himself 'Androuet du Cerceau.' It is by the name of du Cerceau that he is invariably spoken of; but what have municipalities to do with the fancies of artists? Paris has a street called Androuet, after the elder du Cerceau, but no street called du Cerceau after either the elder or the younger Androuet. An earlier Town Council showed more common sense in letting the city have its Rue Molière instead of a Rue J. B. Poquelin.

The system of commemorating celebrated men by naming thoroughfares after them would be more convenient if there were any means of assuring that the celebrity should last as long as the streets. It is a pity for the Street of the Three Brothers to become the Rue Taitbout, the world having long forgotten the existence of that worthy functionary. One day even the Rue de l'Arbre Sec may become the Rue Jean Durand, after a burgher or a benefactor; and away will go the whole history of the Croix du Trahoir (the 'dry tree' of the gibbet and the Crucifix), where men were tortured to death; the whole legend of that Egyptian tree which, in leaf since Adam knew Eden, withered into decay at the moment of Christ's death. We may even have to part from the Street of the Good Children (who studied hard and earnestly), and the Street of the Naughty Boys (who lived by theft and malpractices).

Another drawback to the apparently sensible system of keeping down statues by making a man the honorary (and usually posthumous) godfather of a street is the cumbrousness of some names. It is obviously easier to live in the Rue Lepic than in the Place Jean-Baptiste Clément, especially as the taxi-man has never heard of the latter; and although pre-war dwellers in the Rue de Chaillot may or may not have been acquainted with the interesting reputation of its most disreputable convent, which the earnest Louise de la Vallière herself could not rescue from historical obloquy, they must have been disconcerted, even under the influence of war emotion, to find themselves postally situated in the Street of King Peter the First of Serbia!

There are several puns among street-names in Paris. When Colonel Denfert-Rochereau's heroism entitled him to this honour, the authorities thought fit to give him the Rue d'Enfer; a thoroughfare whose hectic title was not due, as tradition wishes, to a scandalous haunt of mediaeval roisterers and traffickers in black magic, but to its having been the Via Inferior of the Romans. A similar play on words gave Eugène Delacroix the Street of the Cross, and St. Andrew had to share with del Sarto. Towards the end of the eighteenth century the rage for baptizing streets after men became so general that public protests were made, and 'the illustrious unknown' had to curb their ambitions.

Under Napoleon, politics were swept from the street-names in favour of victories and victorious generals. After 1815, of course, all this changed again; also in 1830 and 1848; again in 1870; and in 1915 a French citizen upraised a plaintive voice to know whether, after removing the statue of Berlin from the Gare du Nord and turning the Rue de Berlin into the Rue de Liège, the authorities were going to stop short of sweeping from the streets of Paris the traces of every battle gained by Napoleon on Germanic soil. This was at a time when it was proposed to change the name of the Pont d'Iéna; it was usefully recalled that the last time that suggestion had

53

been heard, Blücher was the man who made it – and that it was not accepted.

There is now, of course, in Paris and all over France, a terrific crop of avenues, squares, boulevards and streets called after Joffre, Foch, Gallièni, President Wilson and other war heroes. Post-war politics having impaired the generosities of war-fever, there have occasionally been 'incidents' in this connection; one fine morning the Avenue du President Wilson, once the Avenue du Trocadéro, found itself name-less – somebody during the night had carefully obliterated the new name. Even so during the Boer War the sun set upon the Avenue Victoria and rose upon the Avenue Kruger.

Many street-names of the past can be read, cut deeply in the stone of the houses above the neat and practical blue rectangles of the Third Republic. The Place de la Concorde still announces itself as the Place Louis XVI; and in some other cases, where streets were named after saints, the religiophobia of the time has furiously erased the Saint and left them merely 'Rue Séverin' or 'Rue André-des-Arts.'

In spite of the general uniformity of house-fronts in Paris, where most buildings are six storeys high and four windows wide, the eye can find oases of difference in which to wander. There are the green settings of villas in Passy and Auteuil – red villas, white villas, yellow villas; villas studded with unexpected blue tiles encrusted with glazed yellow countenances or designs; old country-houses bewildered by the encroachment upon their privacy of urban railings and lock-up gates; villas built for people who must catch the 9.30 tram; villas which reverentially frame the garage of the little Citröen, and villas on which respectfully attends the young palace that houses the Rolls-Royce.

Then there are the avenues between the Bois de Boulogne, the Trocadéro and the Etoile, where all the houses have fixed incomes. Camels have no prouder faces, nor sheep a countenance more stupid. On every frontage can be read the certainty that here are no vulgarians who live without butlers, let alone the crawlers who have to make a time schedule for the bathroom. A Laurel, a Lilac, and a Chauffeur grow round the gravel-sweep; a gardener dresses the first

54

two, and Monsieur's own tailor the last. The Chauffeur sometimes has to be out late, but then the Laurel and the Lilac cannot give notice, so things cancel out on the whole.

But the principal exception to the stiff, dull Haussmann-face of the Paris street is to be found in the cold regards of the old mansions in the Faubourgs Saint-Honoré and Saint-Germain. Never did a dowager at a subscription dance look more haughtily blank than they. They have their lorgnons perpetually to their eyes – and their eyes are closed. They not only do not, but could not, see the approach of anything or anybody not of their caste. Most doors are smaller than the walls in which they are set. This rule is reversed in these quarters; the wall upon the street is as tall as ramparts, but the door towers like a castle. The house itself, of course, is ten or twenty yards away, withdrawn from the vulgar clatter of the gate and the court, so that no butcher-boy or millionaire can get near enough to be offensive. In the huge gates, meant for the passage of such coaches as took Louis XVI and his family to Varennes with a hopeful rumble, and came back with drums and tumbrils in their wheels, little doors are cut – irresistibly reminiscent of Sir Isaac Newton and his cat, and making one feel as small as his kitten. Aged family servants look forth now and then from these impenetrable façades – old men in wasp-striped waistcoats, who are aware that butter is dear as they are aware that Louis XVI has been murdered, but who know, as simply and surely as they know that one does not live if one does not breathe, that the family they serve is as right and as great as its own front door, whether it be the Rochemoreaux de la Beauce or the comparatively mushroom marquisate of the Corrèze de Saint-Paul de la Brière-Roncesvaux.

There is something about these huge doorways, with their curved tops, higher than the walls, and their great knockers (silver faces with silver curls, or interlaced silver snakes, or mere blocks of massive steel or brass in the shape of handles), which satisfies the deep idea of privacy which is characteristic of France. It is the same idea which moves a Frenchman, when he buys a plot of land, to begin his building by putting up two square brick pillars which are intended to support his gates – some day. There are as yet no gates, and the plot is outlined by thin plants, or not at all, or by a couple of lines of unbarbed wire that a drunken donkey would find no obstacle. In this same condition of tall and solitary grandeur the pillars may remain for many a year after Monsieur Durand or Monsieur Lenoir has been in residence; but they represent in his mind the princely seclusion in which any Frenchman would wish to dwell, and which he sees in the great doorways of Old Paris, and even in the high portals of modern houses, when the architect has obeyed the tradition almost sub-consciously. These latter entrances never look taller than when some one in the house has died, and the undertakers have dressed lintel and support in black cloth, with the initial of the departed in white over the middle. During the early part of the War, when the musical profession was finding times very hard, these great doorways served as impromptu theatres, where during the lunch-hour groups of midinettes and clerks gathered to hear vocal and instrumental concerts which were sometimes of a very high quality.

There is one quarter of Paris which, save for its museum, is strangely neglected by visitors – the Marais. The tide of commerce has half-submerged it, and the old courtyards are now occupied by lorries and tricycles; most of them have modern blocks of offices on the street-front. But this is of all Paris, not excepting the Louvre, the quarter where one can realize just how much the grandeur of the old *régime* was imposed upon the daily life of the citizens. Here is the Palace of the Guises and the de Rohans, with a vast courtyard that saw the birth-pangs of Modern France, and now hears the trundling of barrows containing its dusty birth certificates. Here is the mansion in which a loving mother sat down to spend happy hours writing the news to her married daughter – Jean Goujon decorated the walls, Madame de Sévigné illuminated the rooms. These two, the Archives and the Paris (Carnavalet) Museum, are intact; but a score of other historic mansions within a square mile have been given false faces by the surgery of modern commerce. Nobody could guess from the street where to find the monogram of Diane de France (and the fig tree that bears fruit that ripens); the well into which Madame de Brinvilliers dropped the corpses of those she poisoned; the perfect round vesti-bule where Louis XIV, a pompous child, stepped from his coach

56

when he visited his mother's friend, Madame de Beauvais; and who in the world could deduce, from its blank stucco front, that the Billettes school-children clatter to and fro under the only cloister left in Paris until the recent exhumation of the Cloître Saint-Severin?

Some of the doorways of Paris are incomprehensible. In the Rue Visconti, to take one of many examples, the entrances are obviously designed to receive the cumbrous coaches of the period. Nothing could be more practical, only for the awkward fact that the street is so narrow that no coach that size could ever have made a right-hand turn in it. Coachmen, sitting like the League of Nations between the sensitive horses and the high-tempered passengers, must have had to ease a coach where it did not want to go almost as gently and lengthily, as careful of kicks and of scoldings, as if they were modern diplomats. Or else horses and the dukes that owned them were more reasonable then than they are now.

If the house-fronts of Paris tend to uniformity, the shop-fronts are as varied, as gay, as conventional, and as sure of themselves as the mediaeval guilds. It was once a great thing to be a Carpenter or a Goldsmith; but now, if you are a seller of horsemeat, you are just as proud of yourself – you fix in your lintel a horse's head, in purest gilt. And if you sell donkey-meat you put up the head of an ass. If you sell tripe and offal you paint your shop red. It is only sad-minded modern butcheries and charcuteries which have not glazed black panels beside the doors, on which in bright colours are depicted scenes in the lives of the animals now exposed for sale – mutton when it was sheep, and calves before they were veal. There is something sad, almost Euripidean, about going in to buy ham, bacon, or pressed beef between one picture of cows being milked under trees by pretty girls, and another of little pink pigs in a nice clean sty being watched by a young lady and a young gentleman engaged in tender converse.

The wood-merchant nearly always tops his door with a painted representation of the end of a wood-pile. The oil and colourman had his frontage painted in futurist slabs and angles of the primary hues before Jazz was thought of. Only in Soho can London enjoy the fine-laundries as they are known to every quarter of Paris, with their display of delicate underclothing, and their pleasing smell of hot linen, their clack of voices, and their general suggestion that Madame Sans-Gêne will appear at any moment.

A very foreign feature of Continental shops to English eyes is their dedication to some happy aspect of their trade, to its patron saint, to the owner's pet feminine name, or to the topographical situation of the shop itself. Thus one can feed very well at the Belle Gabrielle, at the Petit Coin, at the Trois Portes, or at the Côtelette, where the horrible painted sign (a raw and deeply uninviting portion of a sheep) is an unmitigated libel on the fare. Baby-linen is devoted to special daintiness in a shop called 'Au nouveau-né' or 'Au baby'; only a dandy of the worst kind would refuse to buy his shirts of a firm which coyly announces itself as 'the 100,000 Chemises'; and even French tobacco might be fragrant if bought from the garden-loving vendor who has paid a solid sum to have thick white letters applied to his windows, christening his ordinary little shop 'The Cyclamen.' As for the confectionery which countersigns itself 'The Greedy Child,' it would sell poor chocolate indeed if it failed to command patronage. Even dentistry has a shot at the romantic in 'Le Palais des Dents'; but the illuminated red tooth that throbs outside the very modest establishment is like toothache made visible. How proud a title is that of the enclosure of wooden boxes and aged canvas which the proprietor has christened 'Le Ratodrome!' Dolly Varden's father still, in Paris hangs out a Golden Key above his shop; and the cobbler his order of the Boot.

Some of the brightest spots in the Paris streets are provided by the food shops, which are much better set out than in England. As all earth is removed from vegetables before they are put on sale, carrots and turnips become very decorative items in the scheme of the greengrocer's display; fish lie gleaming on beds of green branches; and, if nothing can make butcher's meat a beautiful sight, there is at any rate a satisfaction in seeing how neatly the best joints are boned and rolled and larded; each, like a prize dog in winter, has a well-fitting overcoat closely fastened around it – in this case of ivory-coloured fat. Many of the barrows are well arranged also. There could not be a more beautiful decoration, even in a King's palace, than that of a costermonger's cart showing purple and golden plums against a tall screen of purple and green grapes slung in alternate bunches on a background of asparagus tops. With the sun shining through the grapes this was like a verse from Revelations.

Flowers are among the loveliest sights of the streets, in Paris as in London. There is nothing like the stolid beshawled women, sitting behind their baskets, as known to England; the flowers are piled on barrows, or set out in tall kiosks, and sold by vivacious Frenchwomen who belong to the great class of the *petite bourgeoisie,* and are far from forming a class by themselves. In these small Edens the seasons are confounded; peonies and roses and stocks and lilies and ranunculus and apple-blossom all bloom together among late narcissi and early gladioli. Here it is hardly an hour between daffodils and asters, but it is certainly a crowded hour of glorious life. There are blooms for sale which appear exotic to the foreign eye; there are homely nosegays from cottage-gardens; but let no dazzled foreigner try to fathom the names by which they are known. There is a different word for daffodils and for cactus-flowers at each kiosk or barrow; you may buy sweet-william, by some happy chance, but if you ask *comment ça s'appelle* you will be told that by her faith the lady does not know; it's something from the country – and she casts a cold metropolitan eye upon it.

On the other hand, the newspaper kiosks, which present a microcosm of the world in the titles of the journals on sale, are remarkable for the almost foolhardy courage with which the saleswomen attempt to pronounce those titles. Le Teemez, for instance, is no stranger to Printing-House Square, though its editor might not recognize this sign of *The Times.*

Apart from barrow-markets of food Paris has a large branch of ambulant commerce. Socks, and lace, cigarette-lighters, lamp-shades, braces, Japanese incense, safety-pins, underclothing, shoes, note-paper, and strips of synthetic sable, are all exposed for sale, whether in permanent lean-to shops, or on temporary trestles set up against the barriers of street-menders. The big drapery houses on certain days sell off similar goods on outside stalls; in the case of single articles the prices are usually the same indoors as out; but in the matter of fabrics the outdoor bargains are really much cheaper than the same material in its own department. By cutting the coupons a little shorter than a dress-length, a little too small for a cushion-cover, a little bit skimpy for a counterpane, the wily ones who arrange these things are almost certain that the woman who has bought four-and-a-quarter metres of stuff at thirty-six francs a metre will return for another two-and-three-quarter metres; will not find them – and will enter the lordly and ultra-modern portals of ground crystal to buy the extra length at forty-eight francs.

At New Year the boulevards are encumbered with booths selling brass, engravings, toys, nougat, and what-not, as most Paris visitors know, as well as they know the slowly perambulating crowds which result. Less-known are the July booths along the not so cosmopolitan boulevards to the east; less still the little Caledonian Market which for a fortnight in July and another at Christmas adorns the hideous Boulevard Sebastopol, and the big one which in Holy Week brings huge crowds to the Bastille Quarter, when the Foire aux Jambons is held. This is no mere name – the first furlong of the Boulevard Richard Lenoir is given up to hams from every part of France that grows pigs; and there are sausages of pig, and sausages that have met an old horse, and sausages that almost bray, and sausages which have married more garlic than ever perfumed Roslin Glen. At the end of this array is the great stall of the biggest horse-preserver of France; decked in silver-clothed cylinders like Zeppelins, all relieved against fir-boughs from the mountains of Alsace (or so let us think), and as pretty as a picture was in the simple old days when pictures were pretty.

Beyond Edmond's booth is the long quadruple line of stalls where old iron and cracked china and dilapidated furniture hob-nob. On March 23, 1918, Big Bertha broke upon Paris in loudness and pain, and all the fearsomeness of the unknown. Until late in the afternoon of that bright Saturday of spring nobody quite knew of what kind this, the thirtieth of Browning's twenty-nine distinct damnations, might be. After a morning hate on the Sunday there was a pause in Bertha's monologue, but about three in the afternoon she began again. Down at the Ham Fair there was the usual Palm-Sunday crowd of roughs and toughs, of dealers and stealers, buyers and spyers. Yesterday morning she had been to them a mystery and a terror; this afternoon, after the physical jump she always produced, she was hailed with 'There she goes! The good old female one!' or 'Hoity-toity, ain't we cross!' or 'You'll feel better now, darling'; and immediately went on again the really serious work of barter for rusty locks, a broken ear-ring, a wooden bed, or two sheets so well patched that the needlecraft was openly vaunted as part of the price. Discussions arose, sometimes of a heated nature, couched in French more picturesque than Racine's; bargains were struck amid wailings of the vendor, grimly-concealed satisfaction of the purchaser; the French crowd, gay, avaricious, business-like, amused, courageous, genial, went on its way beneath a smiling sky that had death in it; and in doing so unconsciously painted that year's Ham Fair with the national colours.

The Foire du Temple still exists – once the Middlesex Street of Paris, now the annex of cheap clothing stores; and on week-ends portions of the fortifications are devoted to the sale of holey sauce-pans and ancient mattresses. Here china and iron may be safely bought; but it will be borne in on the buyer of dilapidated wooden furniture and upholstered sofas that the unpleasing title of 'La Foire aux Puces' is perhaps already a euphemism.

Nobody knows Paris who has not seen her open-air markets. Rigidly policed and taxed, they are nevertheless one of the first things which seem to the ingenuous western visitor a sign of the freedom of life, the generosity of nature, the liberation from convention, of existence in France.

But the most likeable outdoor merchandise of Paris is the book-trade along the river. This has been described, painted, drawn, and commented on a thousand times. Yet it remains fresh to the observer; of all the streets of Paris the Seine is the most romantic, the most interesting, the oldest, and the most modern. Its parapets have supported the elbows of generations of dreaming geniuses; now they bear great boxes of books, where old people, brought to poverty by their brains, stand in shiny overcoats or shinier jackets to finger the books they cannot buy. No ragged urchin whitens his nose on a confectioner's pane as ardently as these pinch-faced folk plunge their eyes into the pages, cheese-coloured with age or fresh as cream, where live the words they want to read. And, in all France, no traders are so slow to ask for money as the booksellers of the quays. Their own poor living comes from selling these pages; but when an old man with green reflections on his brown collar and mirrors on his elbows, comes and stands reading a fifty-franc book, chapter by chapter, day by day, he becomes an honoured guest to the salespeople who cannot understand a word he reads. Immediately underneath him the riverside plane-trees move their shadows over the fishermen, the cranes, the barges, the steamers; a waft of steam, a deep-sea blast from a tadpole tug, bring romance like a smoke of distant ships across the mind; and the sturdy, unmoving Louvre casts into the hurried water a profile as immovable as a proposition in Euclid, as self-sure as a profiteer's son, as transient as the old Notre-Dame that succeeded the altar to Jupiter, as unchanged as the Notre-Dame that has seen twenty-five generations of man die down like the flowering grass.

There is nothing about the Paris streets which more definitely strikes the British or American visitor than the café life on the pavements. This is not particularly Parisian, for it is a feature of European life from Cherbourg to Constantinople, from Stockholm to Algeciras; but as the great body of travellers meets with it first in Paris it is the Paris café which remains in their minds as the typical café – something so foreign that there is no equivalent for its name in the English language. The old English coffee-house was not a café in the modern sense, and it has vanished now. So is also vanishing the Paris café in its most characteristic form. There was a time when the very best thought of France, in the arts and in politics, was to be found round such and such tables in such and such a café. The Frenchman's café was his club. He sat inside it, in an atmosphere that asphyxiated his ardent overseas auditors; or he sat outside it, on nights that froze them; and he explained his thoughts without stopping, having what in French is the *don du verbe*, and in English we have rather jealously diminished into 'the gift of the gab.'

62

"Of all the streets of Paris the Seine is the most interesting"

François Coppée is gone, and his own café has dropped his name from its modernized façade; Ernest Lajeunesse is among the shadows, and the Napolitain now depends for its renown, not upon the distinction of its clients, but upon the fact that the boulevards are being robbed of their cafés by banks and cinemas, and there remains hardly one of the old places where, before a meal, between the acts, or after the theatre, the brilliant men of Paris met to exchange ideas and epigrams. What is left is the cheerful outdoor lounging. Cromwell Road itself would be lively and amusing if people sat about on its wide pavements, drinking lemonade and coffee and queer-coloured drinks that are as mild as French oaths, and as much respected. The cafés of Paris are no longer part of her intellectual life, but they are certainly the chief feature of her streets; on pavements hardly wide enough for a honeymoon couple to walk on, a flimsy chair and an oak-grained tin table will defend against all-comers the right of every good Frenchman to enjoy upon the very streets of the loved city his Byrrh — and Frankincense.

On the smaller cafés remain the white letterings of pre-war days — pathetic testimonies to the lasting nature of that day's work, and to the genialities of life at a moment when coffee really was a penny a glass, and a liqueur cost three sous. These white and shining figures are love-letters from Lethe; we have long forgotten the days when prices so much resembled the violet; and we cannot be angry with a hard-working cafetier who leaves upon his windows promises it would be more expensive to remove than it was to make them.

Paris is a city of vistas, sometimes so well arranged that they seem like happy accident, but sometimes obviously the pet children of expediency. The first are always beautiful, the second are usually handsome, and most of them are tree-bordered. The green whiskers of Paris make most of her pale street-faces good-looking. At twilight the Ecole Militaire, with its lighted esplanade, seen through the giant legs of the Eiffel Tower from the heights of the Trocadéro, has poetry in it; the vista from the Louvre to the Arc de Triomphe is probably the most magnificent of any city in the world; and the Avenue de l'Opéra is really a very creditable commercial thorough-fare, with the Opéra looking frightfully social and well-bred at one

end, and the Hôtel du Louvre discreetly shielding the long mono-
tony of the palace at the other.

Then there are the real accidents which no town-planner foresaw. A fine city has them always in its career, just as statesmen
fall in love. In the Strand (London, Eng.) on a scorching summer
afternoon, when one is immersed in business and hurry like a fly in
hot porridge, one can look down Savoy Street and see the Crystal
Palace shining like a diamond upon the fair throat of the Surrey
Hills. In Paris, when the boulevards are baked whiter than ever,
and the taxis hoot louder, and the omnibuses rumble inside the
head instead of outside the ear, you may see down a narrow street
that begins with a bank and continues with another (and what could
be more unpromising?), an unimaginable pile of churches. There are
only two, but they might be three or six, or a dozen, from the look
of them. There is one, the colour of slate on a cloudy day, which
is as severely classic in its pediment and pillars as only the architects
of the pseudo-Classic could make it. It lies low, and glowers a little.
Behind and above it, almost as though playing leap-frog with it, are
the heaven-blown bubbles, white as pearl, of the Sacré Cœur. They
hang in the sky from the distant terrace of Saint-Germain like the
palace of Aladdin on its aerial flight; they tower over the streets
of Paris as the mountains tower in the twilight at Innsbrück over
some poor innocent soul who has gone forth to buy a piece of tape,
and is met at the draper's doorstep by the everlasting majesty of
the Lord. They are sometimes hard and white, sometimes jet-
black and hard, sometimes a rose-white dream in a rose-red cloud;
they frown and mourn and glow upon Paris. And up the Rue
Laffitte Notre-Dame de Lorette restates, as definitely as the Acropolis,
the theory that bubbles, however Byzantine, are not what a church
should have. A charwoman who should be a great writer, if a fresh
eye and a direct speech count for anything, once told the owner of
a fox-terrier and a Yorkshire that 'as for the tails, straight ones may
be breeding, but tassels is more dressy.' In the matter of churches
those who look down the Rue Laffitte can take their choice, and may
come to the same conclusion.

London river and Paris river are singularly true, each to their town. The Thames has grown a few wonders, such as Hampton Court, Westminster, Lambeth Palace, Somerset House, St. Paul's, the Tower, and Greenwich. For the rest, it has been busy, and shows it. The Embankment and its little patch of gardens are the absent-minded concessions of Father caught in a good humour on a fine Saturday, and saying: 'Yes, my chickabids, you can have this for your very own garden.' But the south bank has to be commercial, for London is a seaport, and its river-front has no time to be bright and leisurely. London did not build Waterloo Bridge to show what she could do in bridge-building, but to let her citizens move freely about their business, even though the fruitful, interrupting river, flowed underfoot. The Tower Bridge has become in the face of London as important as a nose, not because it is something new in over-water arches, but because people had to walk back and forth upon their business just as earnestly as tall ships had to go up and down the river on theirs.

The Seine also has its business, and attends to it. But then part of its business is to be beautiful. Paris lies along the Seine as well as upon it – and shows it by withdrawing herself behind rows of trees, *vert regardant*. A palace, a row of mansions, a mall, heaps of sand and gravel, bridge after bridge, a tower or two, barges, the shifting shadows of plane-trees, and, at every ten yards, a patient fisherman watched by a patient crowd – that is the Seine. Then she has her island, where the temples of worship, of justice, of punishment, and of healing cast into the water their countenances rendered tranquil by centuries of tumult. London's Southwark, where an ancient Cathedral lies hidden behind wharves, like an herbaceous border behind an impoverished old house; her gardens and wharves and cranes that two men as different as Dickens and Whistler could love, are as much London as the Seine balustrades, her book-boxes, her overhanging dwelling-houses and her tree-sheltered palaces and mansions, are Paris.

The Louvre holds out its arms to Paris, and Paris flows into them as the Atlantic flows into Casablanca Bay, and as restlessly turns to get out. There is nothing gentle or restful, let alone homely, about those gauntly handsome arms; they are as aridly and exigently possessive as spinster aunts; and gardeners and mayors have made gardens between them, oases of changing loveliness as beautiful as babies. If only sculptors had been less busy!

Paris is paved in many ways. In the reign of Philip Augustus, the smell of the mud was so strong, even in his palace, that he could not stay at the window to watch the great world go by. In 1185 he ordered his faithful people to lay down 'strong, hard stones.' They did so, just as far as the 'Paris Crossways,' where the old Saint-Jacques–Saint-Denis highway overpassed the Saint-Antoine–Saint-Honoré road. One is still jolted on this spot, because the tramways have points there. Then there are the cobblestones of Louis XIV, of which the best one can say is that they must have been good for the Monarch's digestion; there are fan-shaped pavings of stone; there are tarred wood, and untarred wood; there are oil-smooth asphalts where even the lordliest chauffeur skids somewhere off a-lee. And there are smooth cobbles, which are in many cases so parti-coloured that after rain they look like the paving of the New Jerusalem; there are the road-corners where tram-rails make lines like the Necklace of Venus upon the prostrate throat of Paris; there are spots of the old Macadam.

Parisians are keenly interested in the toilet of their streets. Nearly every gutter is flooded with fresh water and swept every morning. There are so many street-cleaners that neither rain nor snow can take them aback, and the latter is so hastily shovelled into the nearest drain that nobody thinks it worth while to own a sleigh. Only seven years before Queen Victoria came to the throne, Parisians were cutting a fine figure sleighing in the Champs Elysées, behind high-stepping horses crowned with plumes. Nowadays one complains to the Municipal Council if one's car skids.

The lighting of the Paris streets is as foreign as their building. The lamp-posts are tall, and ivy (as bronze as they) twines round them. Sky-signs are slowly spreading from the centre outwards, and the winking fever of the boulevards, which invades your private life as far as your very tooth-glass, or tells you the latest news of the newest stunter, is gradually spreading its incandescent tentacles towards the Arc de Triomphe itself. In 1925 the Decorative Arts

66

Exhibition, which turned the centre of Paris into an Armida's garden of enjoyment, light, and colour, also gave us the Eiffel Tower as a lighted candle to illuminate the dark skies. The enterprising manufacturer who persuaded the State to let him the Eiffel Tower for purposes of publicity had to pay very heavily for the privilege, and even more heavily for the electricity; but Paris has benefited – parts of Paris have; the sequence of gold and silver lines and stars which have turned the tower into a pillar of fire by night, and the great letters which have given us the name of a maker of cars as a golden thought to take to bed – all these bright illustrations of the dark hours are given only to the wealthy quarters of Paris. The other two sides of the tower are dark – including that which might, but does not, shine upon the manufactory in question. Well, it is interesting and pleasing to have the sky illuminated with a vertical solar-system; and it is really wonderful to see the moon taking a round-eyed look at this rival.

She can also look down on a street which, up to 1923, was lighted by oil-lamps. It still has those lamps, hung up against the walls; but the citizens, who have electricity in their houses, have put out bulbs in the street that is still innocent even of gas, and so the old oil-lamps lie rusting against the houses.

The earnest traveller of the boulevards, whether he be charged with the cold and luminous Vichy, the mild and eructive French beer, or the varied and untrustworthy Wischschsky which never saw Scotland nor a barley-field, will get a shock when he perceives two blue and purple bulls slowly uprising against the darkness and slowly butting each other; when their horns meet, a huge electric lamp lights up for purposes of advertisement, to the relief of those who have till that moment supposed themselves victims of hallucination. For, after all, blue and purple bulls. . .!

Among the lights of Paris which one does not forget are the tall kiosks of glass advertising theatre and concert programmes. On Sunday evenings the Paris streets are illuminated here and there in a manner unknown to London – a baker's is open, or a flower-shop; in the Rue de Passy you can buy books long after twilight on a Sunday.

It may be unpleasant for the merchant of luminous signs, proud of his modernity, but it is true, that France had already forbidden them in the Middle Ages – until Henri IV, faithful as ever to the commercial interests of his country, lifted from mercantile Paris a decree forbidding 'all advertisement, all propaganda, which might be regarded as rivalry among confrères.' The medical profession still labours under this interdiction. The luminous signs of those days were oiled-paper lanterns with silhouettes of animals and birds circling inside them. Ah! he would be welcomed, the man who would take from Paris the night-signs which make of her darkness a thing as hectic as her pavements, and as restless. The winking stars now have the air of being dazzled by the rods of intense violet and vermilion light which throb at them. Only late at night does somebody touch the merciful switch that kills them – and the hooting taxicab, bound to Montmartre, the hasty footstep of the real Parisian, are left alone in the foreign-looking streets.

ALL GAUL NOWADAYS IS DIVIDED INTO TWO PARTS. THERE IS
Paris, and the rest, which is nowhere, is contemptuously called
'la province.' Notwithstanding the fact that a large majority of
Parisians comes from country towns and villages, Paris looks upon a
man from Lyons or Marseilles as happy, in that he is French, but
nevertheless worthy of pity as one living far from the sun of her
favour. Humble suburbanites or commuters, always a subject for
mirth in other capitals, are deemed more fortunate than dwellers of
proud and ancient cities such as Bordeaux or Nancy. Neuilly, with
its drab streets and cheap apartments, and its population of clerks and
small business men, ranks higher in Parisian precedence than Rou-
baix, Tourcoing and Lille, with their solid burghers and world-wide
trade.

From an artistic standpoint, this Paris pride is not altogether justified. All French architectural treasures are not to be found in Paris,
nor has all French history there been made. Against the Marais
quarter of mediaeval Paris, Tours can proudly raise her stones and
history. To a Marseillais a Cannebière is worth any Grands Boulevards. Strasbourg, like Paris, was worth a mass. Did not spacious
Bordeaux give a lead, unfortunately but falteringly followed, to
Garnier when he designed the Paris Opera House? The Place Vendôme, with its absurd elongated pepper-castor, is heavy in contrast
with Nancy's Place Stanislas and its delicate ironwork. Paris thus
judged is not peerless. What has made of her the one great city of
France is Napoleonic centralization. She is more completely the
seat of Government – of Government in all its manifestations – than
are London, Washington, and Berlin. Napoleon liked to keep things
under his hand. Self-government as he understood it was government by himself. He constructed all France's formidable administrative machinery so that even its smallest and most distant parts
should be set in motion, stopped and controlled from Paris.

There is the power-house of all Government, the seat of Parliament, the fount of honour, the larder for ambition's greed. Although there are provincial universities of some renown, Paris is a
combination of Oxford and Cambridge, of Harvard and Yale in its
learned supremacy. There are fine municipal theatres throughout

the country, but actors and actresses all come from Paris, and no-where is there even a faint note of challenge to august Parisian insti-tutions such as the Comédie Française, the Opéra Comique or the Odéon. Sandhurst and Woolwich, West Point and Annapolis, are all combined in Paris at the École de Guerre and the Polytechnique. The teaching *élite* of the country comes from the École Normale. The army is officered from St. Cyr, a Parisian suburb. No chemist is worth his drugs unless he has a Parisian degree. No historian has any weight who has not served his apprenticeship in Paris at the École des Chartes. Nowhere else can one study Political Economy. There are a few obscure learned, literary and artistic bodies, with provincial mould thick upon them, but what can compete in majesty and power with the Institut de France with its Forty Immortals, its Academies of 'Inscriptions et Belles Lettres,' of Moral and Political Science, of Fine Arts and of Science? Who was ever known to study art or philosophy elsewhere than in Paris? About the only schools they do not concentrate in Paris are those of forestry and heavy artillery.

In every department of life and its ordering there is similar con-centration. Regional spirit may be strong, local patriotism ardent, but they cannot prevail against Paris, who, like a jealous woman, brooks no rivalry with any of her charms, and sees to it that she gets the best of anything that is going. Who has ever heard of the picture galleries at Lyons or Marseilles, of the museum at Bordeaux? Of course they exist, but to view France's splendid art treasures, taken from the vanquished by a series of renowned collectors from Henry IV to Napoleon, you have to go to Paris. The Beaux Arts every year buy a few canvases from the Salons. When the Luxembourg has made its choice provincial institutions get the leavings, and that in spite of the fact that for years the Luxembourg has been physically unable to give wall space to what it already possesses.

In every field of thought and feeling there is this same concentra-tion. No writer can ever be successfully published except in Paris. No musician can really make himself heard elsewhere. No journalist has any hope of a name unless around him glows the light of a Parisian reputation. No actress is young or beautiful if she cannot claim a Parisian success. Politicians, when they start upon their career of cant and compromise, feel more acutely than most people how important is Paris. Their strength and hopes are founded as a rule purely upon local provincial conditions, for such party political organization as exists in Britain and America is unknown in France.

Young Monsieur Arsène who has fought well, whose father, Monsieur Alexandre Dupont, is known throughout the country-side as a considerate doctor or an efficient 'vet,' presents himself before a constituency with a complete plan for converting France into an eighth heaven. A few old fat farmers, one or two shopkeepers, afraid of Bolshevism, over their cards at the Café du Commerce decide that young Arsène, whose father is a friend of the Minister of Public Works, might not be too bad as a deputy, that he might be able to obtain sanction for the building of that bridge which is going to put money into the pockets of the local contractor and stimulate trade.

All the young man's local past is carefully scrutinized. His affair with Lisette is considered. His attitude towards religion is cautiously examined. It is carried to his credit that he stands well with M. Un Tel, the local manufacturing magnate, with whom no less a person than M. Briand stayed a night a few years before. His radicalism is found to be of a jog-trot and steady gait. He is not a freemason, which in one France means an atheist; nor is he a Jesuit, which in another France means a thief and a liar. He is an ideal candidate, one who may reasonably expect to get votes from both camps, and who will certainly be a political common denominator of the constituency, fighting faithfully in Paris for his supporters' interests.

Then, when all these old gentlemen have got young Arsène already elected, Paris says its word through M. le Préfet. Prefects are mighty and mysterious creatures in the Provinces. In a way they resemble State Governors. In other ways they are Lieutenants of the County. In every way they are more important than these figure-heads of Anglo-Saxon local government. A Prefect is, or at any rate in the eyes of French politicians ought to be, a slave of the Minister of the Interior. In his province he represents Paris, and can if necessary unloose upon his department all the heavy thunderbolts of official disapproval. Nothing can be done without him. His presence or absence makes or mars even a charity sale, and his slight-est movements are controlled from Paris. His influence, which is that of Paris, is all-compelling. Members of Parliament, unless they be solid supporters of the Government which appointed him, are inevitably to the Prefect suspicious individuals whose whispered words and slightest actions have to be scrutinized with care. Constitutionally, it is his task to see to the good administration of his county, to represent Paris on public occasions, to kiss young bouquet-bearing maidens at prize distributions and shake hands with mothers of large families, and behave generally as a younger son of a Royal Family. As a matter of fact, and a fact well known to Prefects – they are in their posts as Ambassadors from Paris.

A French Minister of the Interior has a number of preoccupations which do not worry a British Home Secretary. France has not yet got over her fear of a change of *régime*. In spite of the consolidating effect of victory she still feels that the Republic may be in danger. It is difficult for a foreigner to take seriously such antics as those of Daudet in his Royalist 'Action Française.' Fascist Georges Valois' blue shirts are as unimpressive as Cachin's Bolshevist red garments. But in a country which is the mother of modern revolution, which is struggling with an extremely delicate and vital financial problem, it is but natural that the possibility of a Red, a Black or a Blue dictatorship should be borne in mind. It is the business of the Minister of the Interior to see to it that the country does not falter in its steadfast Republicanism, and in this task the Prefect is the Government's chief electoral agent, and is the only official link between his province and the Central Power. Everything in local life, from the building of a new tram-line to the appointment of a road-mender, is subject to his approval.

If his political sheep happen to bear the outward seeming of wolves in the eyes of the Minister of the Interior, the Prefect will delight in delaying or destroying the pet schemes of those over whom he watches. There will be a pause in the steady rain of decorations with which the Republic irrigates its political fields. Every one will be made to feel the chill of Parisian disfavour. The Deputy will find Ministers deaf and steel-hearted towards the distress caused to the

Department by a hail-storm which in happier days would have certainly meant a vote in relief from the State. Thus Paris keeps a firm hold upon the county and thus Paris strengthens her position as a capital.

She is not only the fount of honour, but also the source of corruption. Parliamentary lobbies are daily filled with the importunate public beggars bred by democracy. Deputies are besieged by them, and Ministers have to hedge themselves round by secretaries and other forms of protection. While the sturdy woman of the fields may laugh at the mincing prettiness of the Parisienne, and the straw-chewing Norman sneer at the pretentious young man from the capital, Paris nevertheless makes herself heavily felt throughout the country, through Parliament and the Press, for just as all teaching is concentrated there, so is Paris the main generating station of public opinion. What Lyons or Marseilles may think to-day is of not the least national importance to-morrow.

The Parisian Press dominates the whole field of national politics, in a manner which is unknown to America, and is only of recent growth in Great Britain. There is practically only one provincial town in France with a nationally important newspaper. Toulouse, with its *Dépêche*, owned by the Sarraut Brothers, has been the chief force behind French radicalism during the last twenty years. There are other important papers in the country, such as the *Petite Gironde*, the *Petit Marseillais*, the *Progrès* of Lyons, but none of them can compete with the *Dépêche de Toulouse* in wire-pulling importance, and none of them can claim the national 'net sales' achieved by metropolitan organs. But even the *Dépêche de Toulouse* has its policy dictated from Paris, where its chief leader-writer is usually to be found. The Paris Correspondent of a country newspaper is by far and away the most important person on the staff.

Only within recent years have the circulations of Paris newspapers been beaten in England, and even to-day it is doubtful whether the five leading London newspapers could produce circulation figures in any way approaching those attained by the Big Five in Paris, and the least prosperous of these to-day, *Le Petit Journal*, could boast of a circulation of well over a million twenty years ago.

Le Petit Journal lost its place at the head of the list as the result of an unpopular and unsuccessful political campaign, and its place has been taken by the *Petit Parisien*, which in Parisian journalism is the nearest approach to a newspaper, in the Anglo-American sense of the word, that France has produced. The *Matin*, the *Journal*, the *Petit Parisien*, the *Echo de Paris*, and *Le Petit Journal*, form the so-called 'presse de grande information.' This term distinguishes them from the swarm of less important sheets which are devoted to the propagation of a particular political faith and have no real commercial existence. They are kept alive either by the brilliance of one or two well-known writers, or by subsidies, willingly granted by or grudgingly extorted from trade or political organizations. For their circulation, they depend almost entirely upon politicians and their hangers-on. But although their readers are few, their influence is considerable, and more than one Government has been punctured by a pin-prick administered by some newspaper, the very name of which may be unknown to the general public. This Press, while ardently read by politicians in Paris, has, however, nothing like the tremendous influence of the 'Big Five' upon the country as a whole.

In nearly every Ministry there is some kind of machinery through which reporters are daily 'doped.' They are told in varying degrees of frankness precisely in what light the Government desires any piece of news to be displayed. Early in the afternoon, the big Paris newspapers go to press with their Provincial edition, so that by noon of the next day the opinions of Paris are making themselves felt in most parts of France.

From a technical journalistic point of view, the Paris Press is extremely badly equipped. Its correspondents abroad are rare, and their use of the cable constitutes an event. Their editorial staffs are, as a rule, so inadequately paid that they have to seek other, and sometimes dubious, methods of supplementing their income. But bad though all these conditions may be, the Parisian newspapers, nevertheless, are a formidable weapon of political propaganda, whether it be in national or international affairs. The ideas expressed in the *Temps* bulletin spread all over the world, as an expression of French foreign policy. An article on finance in *L'Information* or *La Journée Industrielle* gets the same wide-world publicity.

The Paris Press is but one of the many means of Government concentrated in Paris. Its relations with Parliament are even closer than they are in England or in America, and there is hardly a man of any note in Parliamentary life who at some time or other has not been a journalist. Indeed, many of them have won their way from the Editorial chair straight to the Government benches, and have returned again to their desk when out of office. 'Journalism is an excellent profession provided that you get out of it' well sums up the Parisian attitude, and few are the young men who take to newspaper work intending to find therein anything else than a springboard from which they can leap into political life. While Britain and America have produced great editors and newspaper-men, in France it is the polemist who reigns supreme, and Paris journalism is so intensely personal that many of the capital's newspapers depend almost entirely upon the writings of one and occasionally two men for their reputation.

In the 'Big Five' that is no longer the case, although that tradition still lingers so strongly that many people buy the *Journal* solely because of Clement Vautel's 'Film,' the *Petit Parisien* for Maurice Prax's 'Pour et Contre,' and *Le Matin* for Louis Forest's 'Propos d'un Parisien.' These are in no way a reflection of editorial policy, but are the comments of intelligent and witty writers upon some human incident in the day's news. To a certain degree they take the place of the American columnist in the Paris Press. The leading article has practically vanished, save in *Le Temps, Le Journal des Debats* and *Le Figaro;* but let it not be imagined that politics are on that account absent from the other sheets. In the 'grande presse' editorial policy is expressed both in the news that is not printed and in the angle from which every signed writer on the Big Five treats current affairs. The cartoonists are uniformly good. Some of the greatest masters of line, men like Forain and Steinlen, have had their best work published in the Paris Press, and by cartoons as by letterpress Paris is steadily seeking to impose her point of view upon the provinces.

IN NO COUNTRY IS LIFE MORE NARROWLY CANALIZED AND CENTRAL-ized than it is in France. An industrious Frenchman could prob-ably find in close study of the penal code, the constitution, and in the machinery of society a perfectly well-laid course for his every action, from the cradle to the grave. There is almost as much 'Défense' in Paris as there is 'Verboten' in Berlin. The citizens of both capitals come into the world docketed and surrounded by an army of officials whose duty it is to see that they obey, if not the Lord's command-ments, at any rate those of their respective Republics. But while Germans gladly accept all this supervision as a sign of good govern-ment, French people, and Parisians in particular, spend a large part of their existence in finding out ingenious ways of circumventing the laws they have themselves made. The Parisians remain essentially 'gamins' and have ever within them the street-boy's desire to make a long nose at the policeman. Under whatever *régime* he may live, a Parisian is a 'Frondeur.' Clemenceau, who began his political career by serving two months in gaol for shouting 'Vive la République!' as a protest against the mild tyranny of the Second Empire, ended his political life as a ruthless dictator. In the course of his evolution he unwittingly revealed the essential political characteristic of his countrymen, when he exclaimed, as Prime Minister in the Chamber of Deputies, 'I am against all governments, even my own.'

Thus it is that all the supremely logical devices for ensuring good government, invented by gentlemen who have enjoyed the benefits of highly specialized political training, come hopelessly to grief when attempts are made to put them into working practice. If the British Parliament, as so frequently happens, passes into law a badly botched Bill, which is not only stupid but objectionable to the whole com-munity, we have to wait until the legislature has repealed it before we can get any relief. In the interval its provisions are enforced with all the efficient weight of a conscientious civil service. In France they are wiser. It would be a long day's work to draw up a list of laws and decrees, even recent ones, which have never been enforced. Nobody is foolish enough to insist upon the application of a measure which is obviously ridiculous, and the Minister entrusted with its execution just ignores his mandate.

77

It is this mixture of opportunism and common sense that renders so difficult any understanding of French political life. Anyone trying to grasp the scheme of things from the Constitution of the country, its laws or the record of its parliamentary proceedings, would obtain a completely distorted idea of what really happens. Two anecdotes will show the spirit in which the French themselves treat government as a Parisian institution. The first relates to the birth, and the second to the end of a French Ministry:

There had been three or four days of acute ministerial crisis. Matters appeared to be coming to a head, so I went to call upon the Prime Minister of the morrow. The man of the moment had just returned from a day spent in taxi-cabs and arguments with future members of his Cabinet. Inside his private waiting-room was a charming young lady, the 'good friend' of one of the big men in the new ministerial combination. In conversation she sighed out the hope that the new Cabinet would be made that evening and that the list would appear in next morning's newspapers. A few words were uttered to show that the difference that would make to the political fortunes of our mutual friend X was appreciated. 'Oh,' she replied, 'I wasn't thinking about him; you see I've got to go up for my examination at the Conservatoire to-morrow, and the judges know that I am friendly with X, and naturally if they see that he's become a minister I'll pass my examination with flying colours.' X got his portfolio, and the young lady was added to a long list of charming but completely untalented actresses on the French stage.

The other illustrative anecdote was derived from the fall of the same Ministry. I called upon the defeated Prime Minister to express the customary congratulations upon his having got rid of the burden of office. His chief secretary, who was also the power behind the censorship, was engaged in animated conversation with a lady of the music-halls who is internationally known as the possessor of the best-turned pair of legs in the world. A paper called *L'Homme du Jour* had just been suspended by the censorship for some alleged defeatist feature. Unfortunately the blow fell the very week before the usual feature in *L'Homme du Jour* was to have been devoted to the lady with the legs. The sentence of suspension was for three

78

months, and she was naturally upset at having to wait all that time for this bit of publicity. She pleaded with the adamant secretary to let her article at least, appear before sentence took effect. The secretary, while affirming the sincerity of his desire to be of service to his 'chère camarade,' pointed out how impossible it was for the Government to grant her request. He reminded her that the Ministry had already resigned and that it only existed as a Government for the transaction of urgent public affairs while awaiting the arrival of its successor. In such circumstances it would be highly improper to take any decision in such a serious case. While the secretary was thus protecting the dignity of State affairs, one of his colleagues entered the room, and after listening to the argument for a moment or two, slyly remarked, 'Still, I'd do it all the same if I were you; it'll cause any amount of trouble to your successor.' This appeal to the 'gamin' who lurks in the heart even of a Permanent Under-Secretary of State in France was immediately effective; the ban was lifted, and the first row the successor got into was over the reappearance of *L'Homme du Jour* and its subsequent re-suspension.

While it would be foolish to pretend that these two slight stories give a complete picture of the workings of politics in France, they do indicate the existence of a spirit of opportunism and cynical flippancy which frequently leads to surprising decisions being taken.

The cruellest case of the kind in recent times was one in which Clemenceau was concerned when he was Minister of the Interior. Those excitable folk, the southern wine-growers, had been out on strike for weeks, a real leader had arisen among them; police and gendarmerie had failed to prevent the disorder from spreading, troops had been despatched to protect property and restore peace, and it had become evident that the sympathies of many of the soldiers conscripted from the part of the country involved were with the rioters. The situation was extremely alarming when the strikers sent their beloved leader, who was worshipped as few saints are in their lifetime, to Paris, to negotiate with the Government. Clemenceau received 'The Man of the People,' who was a simple, honest enthusiast, unversed in the wiles of government and ignorant of the frightful fickleness of the mob. After discussing the wine-

79

growers' demand, Clemenceau asked their representative to come back to the Ministry the next day for further consideration of a settlement. The man refused. He had to return at once to the South. Clemenceau pointed out that it was his duty to stay in Paris until the last possibilities of peace had been exhausted. Again he regretfully declined, and finally confessed to Clemenceau that the reason why he had to return at once to the south was that he had no money with which to pay hotel expenses in the capital. Clemenceau genially and persuasively at once said, 'Since you're here on the country's business it is only natural and reasonable that the country should foot your bill.' This he joyfully agreed to, and hardly was his back turned than Clemenceau dictated a paragraph for circulation in the Southern Press revealing the fact that the strikers' leader was staying in Paris as the guest of the Government. The cry of 'traitor' arose at once, the adored leader was received with a shower of stones when he returned to his people, and the whole movement was broken.

Perhaps the biggest difference between Westminster and the French Parliament arises from the fact that a dissolution of Parliament is regarded as an extremely grave act, constituting a regular *coup d'état*, and leading to hundreds of streets throughout the country being called after the momentous date of dissolution. That is why Ministries change with such cinematographic rapidity and why the ministerial crisis is almost a stock heading in the French Press. Once a Deputy has been elected, practically nothing but death or revolution can remove him from his seat during the lifetime of that Parliament. He may pledge himself during the elections to giving his electors the moon, and fail after his return to give them even a smell of green cheese, without having in any way to fear the action of any local conservative or radical association. Indeed, there is not a single case of any Deputy relinquishing his seat as the result of pressure from his constituents. He may be elected on an extreme radical programme, and find when he enters the Palais Bourbon that it suits his prospects of political advancement to vote steadily with the extreme conservatives. There is no power on earth to stop him doing it. When a Prime Minister falls, his successor as a rule, in forming his Ministry, has to make a sort of political cocktail

THE CANAL ST. MARTIN

composed of varying ingredients, so as to find a majority in the Chamber. Most French Cabinets are thus composed, with more balancing and delicate thought than the average doctor devotes to the drafting of a prescription.

Thanks to the absence of dissolution as a way out of political difficulties, the Third Republic in its fifty-four years of existence has had very nearly eighty Governments. It is consequently almost impossible to go anywhere in Paris where men of affairs congregate without running into somebody whom you must address as 'Monsieur le Ministre' or as 'Monsieur le Président du Conseil,' for the French politician goes upon the principle that 'once a minister, always a minister,' and even though he may have held office for only twenty-four hours of his life, as has happened to one of the members of the one-day Ribot Ministry in 1914, he would expect to be called 'Monsieur le Ministre' to the end of his days, and as each fresh ministerial crisis breaks out he will look upon himself as 'ministrable' or, as the Germans would put it, in a state of danger of receiving a portfolio.

When those great days of ministerial crisis come, the men who are likely to be called upon by the President of the Republic to form a Government usually affect an air of aloofness from political ambition which is at times comic to those who know how consumed they are with the thirst for office. While they stay at home awaiting the summons to the Elysée, they have a small army of men working for them, picking up and spreading gossip, hints and promises of portfolios in the lobbies of the Chamber of the Senate, in the political cafés and restaurants, newspaper offices and other places where the great game of Cabinet-making goes on. There is but little dignity about the process; the defeated Minister walks out of the Chamber with what grace he can produce, followed by the excited howls and jeers of his opponents, goes to the Elysée and gives the President the collective resignation of the Cabinet. The President of the Republic is bound by constitution to send for the Presidents of the two Chambers and to consult them as to the choice of the next Prime Minister. As a rule, especially nowadays, he also consults the chief party leaders before making up his mind. Then the fun really begins. The first man chosen very frequently knows that he is the last man to succeed in getting a government together, but after taking a few hours in which to consider the situation, he usually accepts the mission. He then sets out on a wild rush round Paris, bargaining with men and with groups, making and re-making formulae which will serve, by their very ambiguity, to persuade the lion and the lamb to lie down together, receiving office-seekers and delegations. In all his excursions he is followed by a swarm of newspaper-men, who are usually older hands in the trade of making Cabinets than the politician himself, and produce a fresh one for every edition of their papers. Nearly all the early combinations fall to pieces, some group or other asking too much, or being willing to concede too little, to the general pool of compromise, and more often than not a dark horse wins the race.

Immediately the Cabinet has been formed, a council is held at which the main lines of policy are laid down; there follows a statement of their policy in both houses, and a general debate which usually gives the practised observer an opportunity of estimating how many days, weeks or months it will be before the same dreary business has to be gone through again.

The frequency of ministerial changes in France not only makes the execution of any big social or legislative programme a matter of extreme difficulty, but also constantly thwarts the efforts of France towards continuity in her international relations. Deputies would think twice before they upset a government if by so doing they realized that they ran the risk of dissolution and the loss of their seats. The immunity they enjoy against such accidents frequently leads to there being almost a complete contrast between public opinion and parliamentary action.

The President of the Republic, whose full term of office is seven years, is elected by the Deputies and Senators sitting together in national assembly in the Parliament Hall of Versailles. His election is attended by as much, if not more, plotting and counter-plotting, bargaining, buying and selling of votes (in a figurative sense) than mark a ministerial crisis. It is one of the rare occasions on which a serious attempt is made to enforce party discipline among all the

Republican groups of both chambers. The day before political Paris empties itself into sleepy Versailles, a Republican caucus vote is taken in the 'Salle des Brosses' at the Luxembourg to choose the Republican candidate for the next day. The proceedings are thoroughly informal; urns are placed on tables along the hall, into which the votes, consisting for the most part just of plain bits of paper with the name of the candidate upon them, are dropped. While the voting is going on, Deputies, journalists, and political hangers-on of every description walk up and down in a cloud of tobacco smoke, feverishly discussing the prospects of their own particular man. When the votes are counted, the tellers, opening the slips of paper, announce whatever name may be inscribed on the slip. An absolute majority of those voting is required, and frequently a second, or even a third ballot, is found necessary.

It is in the intervals between these ballots that the political wire-puller is most actively seeking to swing to his own favourite in the next ballot the votes of a man who has obviously no chance of success. During such a period, when Clemenceau was running Pams against Poincaré as Republican candidate, he seized the President of the Senate, Dubost, by the arm and urged him, as he had only received some twenty votes, to withdraw and advise his supporters to vote for Pams. Clemenceau was loud and vehement, and in spite of Dubost's objections, told everybody that Dubost had withdrawn. 'But,' protested Dubost feebly, 'I must consult my political friends.' Quick as a flash came the brutal Tiger's sardonic reply, 'Political friends! Bah! You haven't got any!' On that occasion Pams was duly elected the Republican candidate against Poincaré; who, although waited upon at midnight by five Radical Republican ex-Prime Ministers, refused to bow to discipline, and presented himself triumphantly at Versailles the next day, when he was elected by a majority drawn largely from the Conservative wing of politics.

Versailles, on Presidential election day, is rudely stirred from its slumbers. It becomes Paris, and is just as important from a social point of view to some people as attendance at the Prix des Drags, or as presence in the royal enclosure at Ascot in England. Already, the Third Republic has its traditions, and lunch at the Hôtel des

83

Réservoirs, built by the splendid King Louis to house the Pompadour, has become a rite. From the mantelpiece in the great white and crystal dining-room, that famous royal mistress presides in marble effigy over a collection of politicians, journalists, actresses, great ladies and great cocottes, who are to the Republic what she and her rivals were to the Monarchy. Every available corner of that hôtel on this day becomes a luncheon-room, and the crowd is so great, the gossip waxes so furious, that any important political conversation can only with safety be conducted behind locked doors. Indeed Clemenceau and Pelletan, when at the last moment they conspired to defeat Gambetta, had to do so in the dark of a housemaid's closet cluttered up with brooms and dust-pans.

While the arrival of so many Parisians in that essentially provincial town gives to it once every few years for a day an appearance of fevered activity, the inhabitants of Versailles, like the rest of their countrymen, are almost completely indifferent to the whole proceeding, and, if it were not for the military display made by the cavalry lining the Paris road, it is doubtful whether anybody would turn up at all to see the proceedings. Indeed, on the occasion of the election of Monsieur Millerand, to succeed the unhappy Deschanel after his tragi-comic fall from the Presidential train, an old lady, whose string marketing-bag was bulging with vegetables, inquired, with wonder in her eyes, why all these people had come to town. She was told that it was for the Presidential election, and she asked again, 'Why, has anything happened to that nice Monsieur Deschanel?' The lack of interest shown by the ordinary Frenchman in the men who rule him is to a foreigner extraordinary. The long procession, of prominent politicians, of people prominent in most other fields of activity, which flows from lunch at the Réservoirs to the Assembly Hall attracts the attention of not a single passer-by.

Yet those who follow politics do so with a degree of passion unknown in our more sober clime. The sombre, dingy Assembly Hall is packed to overflowing by people who have bought, fought, or blackmailed their entrance to see one of the dreariest spectacles imaginable. The proceedings are simple in the extreme: the President mixes the twenty-six letters of the alphabet up in an urn, and the first he draws out denotes that the Deputies of that initial start the voting. Throughout the next two or three hours there is nothing more interesting to see than a dreary procession of undistinguished-looking Deputies and Senators climbing up the steps of the tribune, depositing their votes in a Grecian-shaped urn, and going down the other side of the steps in a hurry to get back to the Salle des Pas Perdus which plays such a tremendous part in every form of activity in France. At Versailles, the 'Hall of the Profitless Paces' is the Galerie des Bustes, where a number of forgotten Generals looks down with marble aloofness upon the fevered crowd of politicians. It is in this Galerie that the first indication of the result is known. It is followed by a rush to the apartment set aside for the new President. There he makes his first public utterance as Chief of State. It is usually of commendable banality.

Nevertheless, occasionally there is a man — as was the case with Millerand — audacious enough to say something at this moment. Millerand on his election declared that he was going to make of the President something more than a dull dummy, more than a kind of Republican Pope, imprisoned in the Elysée. Millerand's conceptions of the real duties of a French President were indeed justified by the letter of the constitution, but no one has yet been found who has been able successfully to put them into effect. With existing Republican organization, any attempt to give to the French President anything faintly approaching the freedom, initiative and leadership conceded to the President of the United States is doomed to failure, as Millerand himself discovered when he was turned out of the Elysée by the pressure of triumphant Radical Socialism.

Millerand, while insisting upon greater freedom for the President of the Republic, especially in the conduct of foreign affairs, was able to refer to the fact that under the existing constitution of 1875 the President is given the power to negotiate and ratify treaties. That power, however, has never been used, and Millerand never at any time found himself able to exert it. Breaking away from tradition, when he accepted his candidature for the Elysée he outlined a programme for constitutional reform, the enactment of which would have singularly strengthened the importance of the Presidential position. Those reforms were designed to put a stop to the constant endeavours of Parliament to meddle with concerns which are rightly matters for the executive to deal with. For that reason he sought to get more than parliamentary sanction for the election of a President, by giving a Presidential vote to delegates of the provincial council, organized bodies of workmen and employers, delegates to the universities, and other intellectual bodies.

Although his audacity in thus putting forward a Presidential programme of such a drastic nature did not deprive him of victory at Versailles, he found himself utterly unable to conquer the suspicion of Radicals and Socialists, who have not forgotten Boulanger and the movement towards personal rule which he symbolized. The day he was elected he spoke of constitutional reform as being an essential condition upon which he took office, but never again dared to open his mouth upon the matter, or indeed to put into effect those rights which the existing written constitution gave to him. His only venture in using the political influence of his office was made on behalf of the Poincaré party on the eve of the election campaign, and led to his being brutally expelled from the Elysée. So long as democracy rules in France, it would seem impossible for any man of marked individuality to be happy or successful at the head of the French Government. Poincaré, who, as Lloyd George and Curzon discovered to their cost, was a man of ability and personality, regarded his seven years' term of office as so many years of hard labour. He, like Millerand, was carried to the Elysée on a flood-tide of popularity which immediately receded, leaving him high and dry upon the Elysian shores. He had been elected with the help of a great many solid catholic Conservatives who expected that he would give dignity to his office and performance to his promises. Within a couple of months of moving into the tawdry splendours of the Presidential palace, Poincaré knew that he was powerless and resigned himself to his lot. As things turned out, the only acts by which Poincaré appeared to be trying to play a personal part rendered him rather ridiculous in the eyes of the Republicans. Immediately after his election, he set out on a round of visits to hospitals, inaugurations of public monuments, and similar functions, whereat his touching a baby on the cheek and his slightest words were chronicled by the Poincaré-ist press with a lavish admiration seldom devoted to royal actions in a country with a democratic monarchy. Clemenceau, still smarting from the defeat Poincaré had inflicted upon him at Versailles, enjoyed this Presidential pomp and circumstance to the full, and was wont to exclaim that he expected any morning to read that Poincaré had climbed to the Colonne Vendôme to look at his 'good city of Paris.'

Although Poincaré fought hard against the removal of the seat of government to Bordeaux on the eve of the Battle of the Marne, and although that move was insisted upon by Joffre, who did not want to be bothered with the responsibility of looking after the safety of the President of the Republic and the whole of the Government as well as that of the capital, he never, as President of the Republic, recovered the blow given to his prestige. His subsequent efforts to retrieve the situation by frequent visits to the troops at the Front were more than stultified by the ingenuity of his tailor, who devised for him something so strangely resembling a uniform or livery that the *poilu* joyously nicknamed him 'Notre Chauffeur National.'

In the hard, logical machinery of the Lorraine lawyer's mind, there was no room for the sartorial psychology shown by Clemenceau, who went to the Front looking more like a tramp than a Prime Minister, and wearing, instead of Poincaré's peaked chauffeur's cap, one of the most disgraceful hats that have ever found their way into history. The hat of Père la Victoire was only second in French affection to that of the Petit Caporal, and it far outdistances all the efforts of our own national mad-hatter, Mr. Winston Churchill.

What Clemenceau would have done had he become President of the Republic in 1919 no one can tell, but it is certain that he would not have belonged to the line of Présidents Fainéants. He did not want to go to the Elysée unless practically begged by the country on its knees to do so. He had himself conspired to make so many Presidents of the Republic uncomfortable that he knew too well what awaited him. His friends, however, urged him with such insistence to become a candidate that he finally consented to have his name put forward at the caucus meeting of the Republican parties, stating at the same time with fine arrogance that he would only accept an invitation to go to the Elysée if it were practically presented to him on a silver salver. His attitude towards the whole thing was well illustrated by a remark he made to one of his young secretaries, to whom he said, 'If I am elected for the Presidency, it's you, my young friend, who will have to serve out my sentence, for I'm not going to live in the Elysée – it would suffocate me.' This attitude upset and alarmed quite a number of Senators and Deputies, for it reminded them of the character and courage of the man they were asked to place at the head of affairs; but such was Clemenceau's popularity at the moment that, had it not been for the intervention of a power greater than any one man – greater indeed than most Governments – Clemenceau would without a doubt have been returned, and a railway signalman would not have known that it was the President of the Republic, Monsieur Deschanel, whom he found wandering along the permanent way in his pyjamas, and whom he recognized for President, so he said, 'because his feet were so clean.' At the last moment the Church threw its tremendous weight into the scales against Clemenceau, and although at the caucus meeting Deschanel beat him by but a single vote, the old anti-clerical tiger knew that he would be caught in defeat were he to go before the National Assembly the next day, since all the Conservatives and the Monarchist block would have rallied to the support of Deschanel.

Fate sometimes displays a grim humour in its dealings with the great, but seldom has it shown itself more bitterly sardonic than in the lot reserved for Paul Deschanel, or 'Poldichinelle,' as the Monarchists irreverently call him. He was a man of Republican aristocracy, a man of letters, member of the French Academy, married to an ambitious woman whose whole career seemed to have been directed towards reaching the Elysée. He had the somewhat florid eloquence that is well received on State occasions in this country. He was good-looking, and the shortness of his stature was redeemed by the magnificence of his moustaches. He was one

88

of the few men who ever wore the livery of the President of the Chamber of Deputies, which is full evening dress, without looking like a waiter. He had no pronounced political opinions and quite enough intelligence to realize the danger of going to the Elysée with any such explosive matter in his trunk.

The differences between the working of the Chamber of Deputies, over which he presided for so many years, and that ruled by Mr. Speaker, are too many to enumerate. Perhaps superficially, at any rate, the most striking is the utter absence of authority on the part of the President of the Chamber, and the utter lack of respect shown to him from the floor.

The Chamber itself is a vast hemicycle, the seats radiating out fanwise to the foot of the galleries for the public, diplomats and the Press. It looks strangely like Covent Garden Opera House, the stage being occupied on the top storey by the Presidential 'fauteuil' and the tables of the secretary, while below him is the tribune from which speeches are delivered. A Deputy, after climbing the steps leading to the tribune, whispers to an usher in black-and-silver uniform with a court sword by his side what particular kind of refreshment he wants to take during his speech – white wine or water – produces the manuscript or notes of his oration, and addressing himself to the House, and not to the Chair, as is the case at Westminster, sees immediately in front of him the ministerial benches. On the extreme left of the semicircle are the Communists, and from there to the extreme right extends a sort of political rainbow which goes from the scarlet of Bolshevism to the true blue of Royalism. Interruptions are the order of the day, and a Prime Minister has been seen more than once leaning back with his arms folded, waiting for as long as a quarter of an hour for a chance to make himself heard even by the shorthand writers stationed immediately below him. To the general chorus of yells the ferocious ringing of the Presidential bell acts as a steady accompaniment. Few men can look dignified wearing full evening dress in the afternoon while violently agitating a dinner-bell, whose brazen voice is about the only one the President of the Chamber has left towards the end of a stormy sitting.

As at Westminster, the hat is given ritual importance, although as members do not wear hats the full Westminster etiquette does not prevail. The President, however, has only one means of suspending the sitting of the Chamber, and that is by groping for the topper, always placed by his side, and putting it on his head. There have been many occasions when the fun has waxed so fast and furious that the House has been suspended several times in the course of an afternoon. A fiery Corsican Deputy has in fury flung the text of his speech – quite a weighty missile, too – at the ministerial benches from the tribune. He followed it up with the contents of the glass by his side, then went the glass itself, and he was about to hurl the salver also when the President managed to get his hat on his head and Ministers were thus enabled to evacuate their benches without loss of dignity. When the sitting was resumed the Corsican was still at the tribune, but as he informed the President that he wished to express regret, silence was obtained for him. He thereupon expressed his regret – that he hadn't got a revolver on him. Again the silk hat came into action and parliamentary proceedings were abandoned for the day.

Since the arrival of the Communists in the Chamber what was left of so-called parliamentary manners has utterly vanished, and hand-to-hand fighting is becoming quite a frequent occurrence. So far, however, the Upper House maintains a somnolent dignity quite on a level with that of the House of Lords.

Eloquence, oratory, rhetoric, or just mere words, play a very much greater part in French parliamentary life than they have done hitherto in our own. It would not by any means be true in France to say that a speech in Parliament had never changed a vote. Owing to the absence of definite party demarcation and party whips, a Government majority is a much more fluid and changing affair than it is in Westminster, where apparently oratory has been, and perhaps wisely, entirely sacrificed to debate. All Frenchmen are good talkers. During the trial of Madame Caillaux for the killing of Gaston Calmette, two of the office servants of the *Figaro* were called as witnesses; following the custom of French courts, the judge asked them to state what they knew about the crime. One could well imagine the sheepish silence that would greet an invitation of that sort addressed to a witness at the Old Bailey belonging to almost any class of British society. These two Frenchmen of the lower classes one after the other spoke for about a quarter of an hour without faltering, both contributing nothing that would be accepted as evidence in a British court of law, but each of them giving a thoroughly plausible account of what they imagined to be the state of mind of Madame Caillaux when she pulled her Browning out of her muff and let fly at the unhappy editor. Among the whole six hundred Deputies of France you do not find one who belongs to the throat-clearing and 'Ahem!' school of speakers so numerously represented at St. Stephen's. There may be many bad speakers among the French, but they can all speak.

Briand has taken himself seriously as an orator, and has worked conscientiously at the development of natural gifts of a deep vibrant voice and an impressive personal appearance. His close friend, that great ornament of the French stage, Antoine, can in fact look upon Briand as being a much more satisfactory production than most of the plays he has staged. Antoine has given real artistic finish to Briand's natural use of gesture, and has taught him just the proper amount of histrionic voice modulation. No one is better at dramatizing the gravity of a situation, or painting the awful perils that are certain to overwhelm France if his Government is upset or if the Government that he is seeking to dislodge is not immediately flung into the outer darkness of unemployment. None can with finer contempt scorn to answer an accusation which it might be difficult to meet in any other way, and none knows better how to use the deadly art of ridicule.

Unlike most great speakers, Briand commands nearly every form of speech, and enjoys the rare quality of never allowing the rhythm of his words to divert his attention from their political object. A year or so before the war I travelled with him to his constituency at Saint-Etienne, where, in a speech which lasted for an hour and a half, he erected the platform upon which Republicans were to fight the next election. The speech was delivered at a luncheon given inside a vast riding-school, which accommodated about two thousand of Briand's working-class constituents. The function was essentially democratic, food was served on bare tables, there were no napkins, the cooking was execrable and the wine was even worse. Briand, apparently having some knowledge of what kind of a meal he was going to get, had lunched beforehand at his hotel, and throughout the meal smoked cigarette after cigarette, running over in his mind the points he wished to make in his address, for he is one of the rare speakers in France who never prepares a note. He was Minister for Foreign Affairs, and posed before his constituents as the servant of Saint-Etienne come to render account of his stewardship. With a grave air of taking 'les braves Stephanois' into his inner confidence, he related all the published facts with regard to the Balkan settlement, with such gravity and such an air of revealing for the first time, and almost in confidence, the inner secrets of diplomacy, that Saint-Etienne was flattered to the depths of its being. Only the little band of politicians and newspaper men who had accompanied Briand from Paris saw running through his speech the first outlines of a programme, and a new political party that afterwards fought the election under the title 'La Fédération des Gauches.' It was in this speech that Briand first separated himself from Caillaux, when, with right hand high uplifted above his head, with his left arm stretched in front of him defensively, he characterized Caillaux as a 'demagogic plutocrat' who pretended to stab Capital in the back while defending it in reality.

Briand has performed at the tribune of the Chamber a one-act, one-man play which lasted for about ten minutes, and saved the Government from an extremely awkward debate. Like every other French Prime Minister during the war, he promised the House that the political censorship should be abolished, and like every other Prime Minister he had failed to keep his engagement. The Ministry was threatened with an adverse vote, and the House was in an extremely bad temper when Briand, moving in the restricted space of the tribune, acted a little comedy in which he alternately played the part of a journalist submitting an article to a censor — whom he also portrayed — and of himself as Prime Minister being consulted by the censor. The thing was done with such comic art that the House forgot its grievances and rocked with laughter.

Clemenceau's speech on assuming office as Prime Minister during the war, when he appealed to the peasants at their ploughs, the workmen at their lathes, to the very babes in their cradles, to realize that they all formed part of the army seeking to oust the invader, would have made Michael Angelo envious of its modelling, Rembrandt of its colouring, and Wagner of its tone. Clemenceau could not pretend to compete with Briand, Viviani or Jaurès in dramatic eloquence, but he was the only master of debate amongst them – not the mild-mannered debate of St. Stephen's, but the stab and rapier-thrust of ridicule and sarcasm. Even as a young man his speeches had nothing of easy grace about them; they all bore the virile mark of the chisel, and were as different from the rest of oratory as are Rodin's volcanic marbles from the placid art which decorates our chocolate-boxes. His speeches were not mere words, they were battering-rams upon human stupidity.

Poincaré is a man whose spoken words read infinitely better than they sound, and by so doing reveal the ex-President's method of preparing his public utterances. He is gifted with an astonishing memory and a colossal capacity for work. It is his boast that, once he has written a speech out, he will still be word-perfect in it a month afterwards. Every single speech he makes he has himself written out beforehand in his fine and not very legible handwriting.

The method has its drawbacks. Shortly after he became President of the Republic he went on an official motor-tour in the centre of France. The programme was extremely heavy, and he had to make an average of at least three speeches a day in the various towns and villages through which the cortège passed. All those speeches Poincaré had written out before leaving Paris, and, relying completely on his memory, he had not even troubled to bring the manuscripts along with him. All went well for a day or two, till unfortunately, owing to a breakdown in the arrangements, one of the villages where he was to speak was skipped. But nothing could upset Poincaré's implacable memory; he remembered the next speech he ought to have made and duly delivered it at the next stop, praising with a wealth of knowledge the achievements of the local great man, who, however, unfortunately belonged to the last stopping-place in the pro-

93

gramme. It took about two days to correct the machine-like work-ings of the Presidential memory. He has a hard and rather disagree-ably resonant voice, his delivery is cold for the most part, but he suffers from occasional vicious outbursts of irritation.

These also are a feature of Caillaux's speech-making, for the would-be financial saviour of France would appear to have that fashionable possession, a high blood-pressure. His almost completely bald cranium acts like a barometer in the Chamber. The approach of stormy weather is announced by the dome becoming delicately pink; it deepens in colour until, when the storm bursts, it is violently purple. Caillaux, who declares himself to be a great democrat, is at the same time extremely proud of his Norman descent; in fact, he claims that the fact that one of his ancestors went over to England with that large party of Norman tourists personally conducted by William the Conqueror is sufficient proof that he cannot be an Anglophobe. He speaks English well, but the French inability to pronounce an 'h' gives him a Cockney note comic in a man of his culture. No doubt as another denial of his alleged anti-English sym-pathies, Caillaux is one of the rare Frenchmen to sport an eye-glass. When at the tribune he fingers it with the ardour of a *dévote* telling her beads. In appearance physically he lacks dignity, but counter-acts his resemblance to a rather cheeky cock-sparrow by an impatient arrogance which at times leads his voice to break disconcertingly at the most impressive moment of his perorations.

Now that death has stilled the voices of Jaurès and Viviani, the extreme Radical and Socialist parties have no great speakers. Pain-levé is completely ineffective. On the few occasions when he says anything, he does so with such a complete lack of fire, conviction, or energy as to leave his audience completely in the dark as to what he means. Herriot is infinitely better, but his air of being a genial pork-butcher makes it impossible to give him a place among really great parliamentary speakers.

Although speeches play a prominent part in Paris parliamentary activity, although a vast amount of the work of running the country is done in the informal atmosphere of the lobbies and at the 'buvette,' the real parliamentary mill is formed by the big permanent committees to which every Bill is referred before it comes before the House. These committees are practically pocket editions of Parliament itself; each one is formed of forty-four Deputies elected on a proportional basis by all the groups in the Chamber with the exception of that which, with a fine sense of humour, calls itself the 'Group of the Ungrouped.' These committees grind out a vast amount of literature. When a Bill comes before them a reporter is appointed, whose duty it is to make an exhaustive study of the question raised by the proposed Bill, and to carry on negotiations with the Ministry whom it concerns on behalf of the committee. These committees can summon any Minister before them, and it is becoming increasingly the practice for Ministers to keep these bodies thoroughly informed with regard to current developments. So much is this the case to-day that when a Minister goes before the Foreign Affairs or National Defence Committee its members are asked to take an oath of secrecy, and as Communist members refuse to give any such pledge, the committee adjourns and an informal meeting is held elsewhere, wherefrom Communists are excluded, sometimes not without difficulty.

On one occasion, when Painlevé desired to give the Foreign Affairs Committee a confidential account of his visit to the Riff Front, and of the progress of negotiations with Spain, the Communist members of the committee were only kept out of the informal meeting after a violent bout of fisticuffs. Nearly all the big men in political life have served their time on such committees, and to be elected either president or reporter of any of the 'Big Four' which deal with finance, foreign affairs, national defence and home affairs, is to become heir-apparent to a portfolio. The training this committee work gives to French Deputies is extremely thorough, for, while in dealing with Bills of a non-controversial character the reporter usually relies upon the services of a permanent official in the Government office concerned, big political questions give to the ambitious young politician an opportunity of displaying whatever gifts of statesmanship he may possess. Perhaps the most notable instance of this is furnished by Briand, who, as reporter on the Bill for the Separation of Church and State, made a reputation as a skilful negotiator and a far-seeing statesman which has made him the recurring Premier of France.

If in England it is the steady reliability of Permanent Under-Secretaries and other high Civil Servants that makes it possible to mould a Chancellor of the Exchequer over-night out of a man who is always worried by 'damned dots' of decimals, or to have as Minister of Foreign Affairs a man who knew nothing of Europe at first hand, in France it is the long schooling received in these committees that qualifies the politician for office; while an English Minister frequently has to learn the workings of his Department after he has taken office, his opposite number in France has usually for years been prying into every activity of the Department which he is called upon to administer.

Most people feel rather mysteriously flattered when they are given the title of Parisian. It is a citizenship that conveys a tribute to one's intelligence and charm, together with a hint of delightful wickedness. It is an elusive quality rather than a civil status, and every Frenchman knows that there is no surer way to the smiles of an American magnate, of an Indian potentate, or of any woman, than to tell them that they are 'truly Parisian.' They will disclaim their right to such an honour, but they will always deny it with purrs.

It is difficult to say who and what constitute the 'vrai Parisien.' Mere geographical accident of birth has nothing to do with the matter. It is more a frame of mind than anything else, and it is easier for the Maharajah of Kapurthala to claim to be a 'vrai Parisien' than it is for M. Arsène Dupont, whose family has sold groceries at the corner of our street for some 150 years. In this respect, Paris has not changed much. It would be foolish to blame upon democracy the dominant position occupied in Tout Paris by exotic plutocracy and aristocracy. Did not the Demidoffs and Soltikoffs, the Lords Henry Seymours and Hertfords, stand out even amid the social glitter of their earlier days? Then, as now, a place in Tout Paris could be bought by extravagance, by gambling, by horse-racing, by the beauty of your mistresses, or by shining eccentricity of manner. Few Frenchmen have nowadays the bad taste to compete with the rajahs and 'rastas,' pork-packers and profiteers, who, making of Paris their playground, give to it a reputation for frivolity, folly and fragility, towards which its inhabitants do but little to contribute.

There is no Court, there are no ruling Duchesses, and the Republican Hierarchy does nothing to take their place. Any President of the Republic would be ill advised who endeavoured to reproduce even a Republican reflection of Monarchical or Imperial glories at the Elysées. Entertaining in the dull home of the Chief Magistrate is purely official and political. A Ball at the Elysée fills all the neighbouring cafés in the Faubourg Saint-Honoré, the Rue Royale and the Champs Elysées, with thirsty democrats who have been unable to find the Presidential buffet. Society, or rather those sets of Bonapartists, Orleanists, and Emigrés Américains who consider that in the Faubourg Saint-Germain and the Etoile they form Society, are not on calling terms with the Republic. The President is doomed to the company of his former colleagues of the Chamber or the Senate, judges, and other high officials of State, and their wives. He has a thoroughly dull time, while the wealthy guests of France enjoy themselves at Monte Carlo, Cannes, La Baule, Deauville, Le Touquet, Aix-les-Bains, Vichy and other perches where 'le vrai Parisien' is to be found fluttering around the race-courses, casinos and doctors. 'Sem' is the only author of the Debrett of 'Tout Paris.' Unless you have been caricatured by his cynically agile pencil, you have striven socially in vain. You may try, but little funny-faced M. Goursat, who has almost forgotten his real name, alone can give you canonization. If 'Sem' has not drawn you, it is as though you had been married in a Registry Office. His album of caricatures is a better social guide than the Blue Book, and it is infinitely more amusing and informative. 'Sem' does not handle his willing sitters with kind pencil. Most of them are foreigners seeking their naturalization papers from Sem's ironic art. There are a few Letelliers, Citroëns and other profiteers, but the majority of 'Sem's' 'vrais Parisiens' have acquired their citizenship in other ways than by the success of a newspaper or the manufacture of a motor-car.

To be Parisian, it is not necessary to have been born within range of the boulevards. A Parisian is a man or woman possessing a difficultly definable mixture of dash and chic, of intelligence or eccentricity, and an acute perception of the value of the right kind of advertising. The late M. Duval, the Childs or Sir Joseph Lyons of Paris, got his freedom of the city by persistently wearing a rounded felt topper over a coachman's side-whiskers. The late M. Arthur Meyer was only accepted by Paris after he had made the whole town laugh by his solemn baptism as a Christian at the Madeleine. Mr. Berry Wall, the old-time Beau of Fifth Avenue, took out his naturalization papers by steadily wearing a Gladstone collar, a floppily tied flowing scarf, and a red chow. Yet all of these gentlemen would probably in a moment of frankness confess that they had social peaks still before them.

Society in Paris has cliques and sets, and while foreign society makes more noise, it cuts no more ice than the local brand which keeps itself, on the whole, rigidly aloof from foreigners and other such innovations. The fact is, that Society, the capital-*essed* kind to which Great Britain is accustomed, with its rules of precedence, Lord Chamberlains and other barriers, does not exist in France. Every socially minded person, therefore, has decided that his or her particular environment, whether it be of the Faubourg Saint-Germain 'Noblesse Oblige' variety or the American Etoile kind of 'Largesse Oblige,' constitutes society. The contempt of the one for the other is immense. The old Royalist people seldom go out. Financially they can't afford to, any more than can socially the new plutocrats, who, however, make occasional landings at Montmartre, and behave with an insolence of white waistcoat which frequently gets them into trouble.

Modern plutocracy has no manners. It seems as little able to digest its oats as is modern democracy, which views all this squandering of money with a yellow eye.

Meanwhile, unsuspected by the world, there exists a real Paris, which is quite other than that of the 'vrai Parisien.' Paris is the busiest industrial city of France. Her administrative boundaries are formed by Vauban's old fortifications. Her real existence spreads out to a red ring of industrial effort and Bolshevism.

It is customary to think of Paris as a city which produces perfumes, frocks, pictures and doubtful novels. Yet it has its industrial life as grey as that of any manufacturing town. The absurd nonsense of Murger's *Scènes de la Vie de Bohême* still colours the foreigner's view of the hard-working young midinette. Paris is looked upon by the foreigner as being a place where labour is a matter of light-heartedness. The most superficial inquiry into the question of hours and wages will remove that illusion. The process of adorning woman is as much a factory trade as cotton-spinning, and to the workers not half as lucrative. Madame, who admires her frock upon a swan-like mannequin, usually has no idea of the insanitary conditions under which it has been produced, with seamstresses crowded

99

one upon the other in low-ceilinged, ill-ventilated workshops. Nor does she realize that the superb creature who swoons round the show-room in the very latest model, when she leaves her business usually does so in very plain and unambitious garb.

There is also a lot of false romantic sentiment about the manufacture of perfumes, which is an important part of the Parisians' activity. You are asked to believe in a beautiful picture of roses or orange-blossom being delicately persuaded to give up their subtleties by young ladies at Grasse or some other ideal spot on the Riviera. As a matter of cold fact, while some scents do come from the sunny Riviera, the bulk of them is manufactured in extremely prosaic factory buildings in suburban Paris, out of mysterious chemical products such as ionine (violets), tupiniol (lilac), vaniline, heliotropine and coumarine.

Frenchmen have managed to make real mysteries out of very ordinary crafts.

There is apparently no limit to the nonsense that can be absorbed by the foreigners with regard to wine, food or dress. These form a large part of Parisian industry. There are nearly 10,000 hotels in Paris, of which certainly 9,000 are bad, and boast of having one bathroom and gas on every floor. But such is the charm of novelty that British, and, in a lesser degree, American, visitors put up with dirt and discomforts in Paris which they would not tolerate at home.

The *patron* or the *patronne* is so polite and so French, that bad coffee, which in France is almost as prevalent as it is in Great Britain, bad service, bad rooms, and even bad food, become an almost agreeable part of the foreign atmosphere. Yet this exploitation of the foreigners is not run on atmosphere. Behind the charm of the *patronne* there is the whole elaborate machinery of modern accountancy, costing and profits. The bell of the cash register is heard through the land.

We are a long way from Mr. Berry Wall's flowing cravats. Nearly 2,000,000 Parisians don't wear any at all. They are the folk who in the Paris area produce 80 per cent. of the motor-trade of France. At Neuilly, Billancourt, Asnières, Suresnes, in the red ring of industrialism and of Communism which encircles Paris with

"A long way from Mr. Berry Wall's flowing cravats"

a population running to over a million people, work is just as hard as at Sheffield or Pittsburg. It is not the Aga Khan, but the butcher from Belleville, who is the real Parisian; it is not Captain Jefferson Cohn, whose colours shine triumphant at Longchamps and Deauville, but the decrepit old fellow who flogs a music-hall horse in the shafts of a fiacre.

The Parisian, in spite of all the false glamour cast upon him by sentimental romantics, is a hard-working, bus-riding, tube-taking man or woman who has not got much, if anything, more out of life than his opposite number in New York or London. He spends much less, but gets more, in his café than the Briton does in his public-house. Dupont takes his money back to Mother with perhaps more regular fidelity than does 'Erb Smith. He is encouraged to do so by the Parisienne.

It is customary to imagine that the female inhabitant of Paris is, by right of citizenship, better-looking and better-dressed than any other female. She is credited with eternal youth, with chic, with 'je ne sais quoi' and other mysterious qualities that bring the males of half the world to her feet in illicit adoration. She is thought to spend her life wearing bold frocks in a way that her less favoured sisters of New York and London cannot hope to imitate; to be daring even in her lingerie; to be naturally witty and accomplished, and equally good at turning an omelette or her lover's head – for as every Paris male has to have at least one mistress, so the Parisienne must of necessity have at least one lover.

This is not, thank Heaven, an essay in comparative morality. It would be easy to contrast a Putney Pecksniff's horror over the prevalence of the nude in Parisian music-halls with M. Dupont's bewilderment over the occasional glimpses he gets in his *Journal* of Hyde Park at night. To the Parisians, the Londoner and the New Yorker are hypocrites. Frank themselves, they see no reason to deny sex, and utterly fail to understand the minds of men who in their own countries appear to treat the matter as being either one of the higher mysteries of life or one of its lower vices. Their bewilderment is naturally increased when they see those same men pouring up to Montmartre and exhibiting themselves with a class of woman whose very existence they both ignore and deplore in New York or London. Nearly all that side of Paris exists for and by the foreigner. It is the rarest thing to see a Parisian in any *boîte de nuit*.

To begin with, the French Parisian does not like to pay 200 or 300 francs for a champagne which is really worth about thirty or forty francs, and which has been so doctored for the Anglo-Saxon palate as almost to burn that of the Parisian with its dryness.

Nor does a lavish display of feminine allurements make any special appeal to him. Thrift in money matters produces a certain prudence in all affairs of life. Present-day Parisian morality would without question fail to meet with the approval of the late Dr. John Knox. With the French, as with all Latins, women do play a large part, for the Frenchman is a frankly passionate animal, and is neither ashamed to admit it nor afraid to shoulder the risks consequent upon that admission. As R. L. S. discovered, folk do live upon the slopes of active volcanoes and fearfully carry umbrellas if the sky be overcast.

In the same way many French Parisians lead curiously exciting existences upon the knife-edge of tragedy, retaining nevertheless all the while a sense of family obligation that would make fall the eye-glass of the youngest of younger sons of England. Family is the sheet-anchor of the French man and woman. Every now and again a young rip makes a fool of himself in the special Paris designed to give the foreigner a sample of French 'gaiety.' He 'posters' himself with some well-known music-hall siren, plasters her with jewels, goes to Montmartre with her. They are seen together at Deauville. But unless the youth be quite specially gilded in his own right, long before he is ruined the family steps in and summons hot-blooded youth before Old Wisdom's bar. For your elder son does not exist in France. All children have their share in the parental estate, and if a member of the family kicks extravagantly over the traces a dreadful Vehmgericht awaits him, in the shape of a judicial counsellor appointed by the family, without whose approval Mlles. Fifi, Toto and the rest can love in vain. Such cases are comparatively rare. The young Parisian of to-day is a serious-minded fellow. He may flirt with Lisette or with Communism much as young Oxford occasionally flirts with its bags and barmaids, but the splendid realities of war, no less than the empty illusions of peace, have taught him, perhaps before his time, that, after death, life is his gravest problem.

The Parisian youngster may have an occasional flutter at Montmartre or Montparnasse. His real home is in the Lycées, the Sorbonne, and the three great Universities of France, the Ecole Polytechnique, the Ecole Normale and the Ecole des Chartes. From them are recruited the men who, conquering a complicated political machine, become great administrators, Marshals of France, builders of Empire, explorers in science, historians and Academicians.

Youth in every country has its fads, fashions, and its special label. Most middle-aged Parisians, wherever they may come from, were brought up amid the dying romanticism of Victor Hugo and the still-born realism of Emile Zola. In their youth they were far enough away from 1870, as well as from 1914, to be able to look upon life through literary spectacles. The calm routine of a civil service offered them all a safe and respectable haven from prosaic troubles about their daily bread. At the same time it gave leisure for writing, for philosophical speculation, a well-dowered bride, and an end covered with the red ribbons of the Legion of Honour.

To-day, the Parisian student is a quite different being, and a much more hopeful portent for the nation's future. Napoleon twitted the British with being a nation of small shopkeepers, and he himself created a nation of petty functionaries. To get employment under the Government was before the war the aim of every right-minded youngster of the middle and lower classes. Nowadays, for posts which formerly attracted hundreds of candidates, there are practically no aspirants.

Government service is not only very badly paid, but, what to Parisian youth of to-day is more important, while it gives a certain social position it does not produce results.

The young Parisian is become in a way American. He no longer wants to record in verse the liquid notes of the nightingale. He wants to grow mahogany or cotton in French Equatorial Africa. Movements of exchange interest him much more than the antics of Petronius or the love-affairs of Casanova. He is become a real realist.

103

In sciences chools white-bearded, mystic-eyed professors agree in deploring their pupils' flight from pure to applied and industrial science. They take no interest in any branch of science which has not an industrial or economic value. Mathematics they put up with as being a regrettable necessity, but consideration of Celestial Mechanics bores them to the point of yawning. Classes in physics and chemistry, on the other hand, are eagerly followed. Younger boys at the Lycées show the same spirit. They, like their elders at University, are aware that war has ravaged what family fortune there may have been, and like them are anxious to rebuild it. They want to equip themselves for work as quickly as possible. They have no time for their books. They want the 'goods' as quickly as possible.

This marked tendency in the home of French education recalls a conversation with Ernest Lavisse, the historian of the Republic and the man who taught the generation of Verdun. Before the war Lavisse, comparing British and French methods of education, argued that France and Britain might with advantage exchange their educational systems. In Britain, we have produced by a marvel of muddle-headedness exactly the type of youngster required by a rapidly expanding Empire. Our school system, if it ever had a thought, has never worried much about the brains of the raw material confided to it by anxious parents. Learning as such has been at a discount. Let the young barbarian develop his body and his character. Young gentlemen do not require brains. Manners, and a standard of some-what obtuse uprightness founded upon tradition, upon code, upon a mute or at least a shamefaced sense of family and wider social duty, have, under this system, provided Downing Street and Charles Street with the amazing youngsters who have pushed frontiers farther and farther into the heart of Africa, and pacified and ruled over areas vaster than England. Lavisse felt that the days of such youngsters were passing; that Britain in the Colonial field had bitten off all she could chew; that now her problem lies in the proper exploitation of the territories she has acquired; that although character is always useful, acquaintance with political economy and with industrial science is also requisite.

Paris – and in educational matters Paris is France – appears to have sinned in the other direction. Generations of youth have passed through her schools and come out full of the classics, all with a strong literary bent, all qualified to be excellent schoolmasters, or, if from the science side, to be satisfactory laboratory assistants or competent industrial chemists at low salaries. To-day France, with her huge North African Empire still to be brought completely under control, wants our lads of character to act as administrators and sub-commissioners. At present it is in the Army alone that she finds more or less the right type of man, for the Civil Service is stocked with bad littérateurs who make but unimaginative bureaucrats.

Already, however, the youth of Paris is straining to meet the demand for the required type of Colonial servant. The young Parisian wants to do things, and is not content to talk about the deeds or words of other men as were his predecessors of twenty years ago. They are much more alive. In literature and in art they are experimental, but practical, and prefer Kipling and Farrère to de Musset or Baudelaire.

Politically, the young Parisian has responded with all the generosity of his immaturity to the call of Mussolini or of Lenin. He is either Action française or Communist – Royalist or Bolshevist. It is perhaps a good sign. Youth is still sane when it has generous notions, and the young man who believes in the restoration of a Monarchy and of a family which brought France to bankruptcy and disgrace shows at any rate that he has ideals. Royalism in France is a psychological stage in a young Frenchman's development, just as Marxism was twenty years ago. Under the guidance of that amazing man Léon Daudet, who writes like an angel and thinks like a lunatic, with the advice of an implacable logical historian, Charles Maurras, Parisian university youth has accepted the doctrine of Monarchism with an enthusiasm which perhaps does really hide a deep-rooted scepticism as to the possibility of a Bourbon restoration. Young student Paris sharpens its intellectual teeth upon Maurras and Daudet, or upon Communist Cachin and Socialist Léon Blum. It has no use whatever for any shade between Royalist sky-blue and Bolshevist blood-red. All the anaemic tints of the extremely Con-

105

servative Radicalism which has hitherto provided Government in France say nothing to the youth of to-day.

Nearly all the Baldwins of French *bourgeois* politics have started in extremist parties. On one occasion Field-Marshal Pilsudski, Commander-in-Chief of the Polish Armies, visited Paris officially. He was met at the station by Aristide Briand, who for the seventh time was Prime Minister of France. Briand conducted this distinguished guest of the French nation to dinner with the President of the Republic, then M. Millerand. The dinner was very official, and Briand over coffee tried to enliven matters by recalling to M. Millerand, President of the Republic, a Conservative, and the cherished hopeful of Duchesses, that they had all three met before. Millerand's memory failed and he put questions, 'When?' and 'Where?' 'Oh, at Amsterdam,' replied Briand, 'when we were all three delegates to the Congress of the 2nd Socialist International.' 'You see,' added Briand, 'what we get out of Socialism. Here's Comrade Pilsudski, a Field-Marshal. You are President of the Republic, and I am the recurring Prime Minister of the country.'

Youth is the same all the world over in exploring extremist ideas. Partisans of political orthodoxy at Oxford worship it with an intensity that is almost as fanatical as that lavished upon the Communist creed by men whose minds are cast in a different mould. But in the explanation of the undoubted influence of Monarchist and Communist preachers over Young Paris to-day, there is more than the natural tendency of youth to excess. There again is sounded the note of realism, the desire for action. With examples such as those of Mussolini and Primo de Rivera, of Coolidge, and in a minor degree of Stanley Baldwin on the one hand, and of Lenin on the other, before their eyes, the youth of Paris schools and university believes in firm authority. Neither Communism nor Royalism will eventually satisfy these lads and most of them are probably already aware of that fact. But for the time being, they feed the youngster's desire to be up and doing. It gives him a thrill to be a member either of a Communist or of a Royalist Centurion, to carry a loaded cane, to wear a blue or a red sash round his middle, and to demonstrate for or against that curiously litigious person, Joan of Arc. Authority has to pre-

106

tend to take its Paris youth seriously. But remembering themselves in their own salad days the grey-headed politicians of the Ministry of Interior do no more than pretend. They know that all that kind of effervescence is bound to die a natural death. They can also congratulate themselves upon having much less of it to quell than had their predecessors, for your young man of Paris to-day is out to make money.

SOME OF THE MOST ATTRACTIVE VILLAGES IN FRANCE ARE IN PARIS. One can sit on a bench, or outside a café, and see the notary, and the oldest inhabitant, and the ambitious young doctor, and the local gossip, all going about their affairs among playing children, whose mothers sit sewing under the trees of the village square till it shall be time to go and hang the cooking-pot over the log-fire, so that Baby Bunting's father may be rewarded for his hunting. Perhaps the fire is a gas-ring, and he has brought nothing more like a rabbit-skin than a promise of a rise in salary 'later on'; but that is a warm wrap for Baby Bunting too; and a fine thing to tell the other Madame Buntings to-morrow, when the babies are solemnly playing in the dusty paths – for under the Republic of fraternity and liberty, grass – a difficult growth in France – is a decoration not to be profaned by the public foot.

Great green and cream-coloured omnibuses lumber by, bearing on their sides romantic names of the strange, far countries of Paris: Opéra, Bourse, Arsénal, Filles-du-Calvaire, Pigalle. There is a fascination in wandering round a big Paris railway station and seeing some huge train ready to start for the ends of the earth, or in standing on a country platform and watching it thunder past, its flanks hung with the most wonderful names in the world: Paris–Vintimille–Rome; Paris–Vienne–Buda-Pesth–Constantinople; Paris–Londres; Paris–Verone–Venise. In some degree the villagers of Paris enjoy this sensation when their omnibuses or tramways go by. They feel at once the pride of the metropolitan and the complacency of the countryman when their placid afternoon is set to music by the gongs and bells and drumming wheels of vehicles which start from a little provincial *Mairie* and stop in the shrieking delirium of the Bourse.

In these villages one never knows what strange figure may alight: an old peasant-woman bearing a basket fragrant with healthy young onions, a chicken's head, deplorably bedight with blood, hanging from under the lid; or a terrific gentleman in black, with gloves on, carrying under his arm a flat mausoleum of black leather full of papers; or a lady wonderfully turned out by the three-colour process, clicketing on high heels; or just old Monsieur Durand from next door, with a chocolate in his pocket and a bit of gossip on his tongue; or a peony-coloured wagoner with a glance as far-away though not as bright as a sailor's, coming from the farms to see the local horse-dealer, with a message from his master involving ten words of delivery and a million of discussion.

The nearness of the country is one of the strange delights of Paris unknown to the sort of visitor who thinks that the olive-coloured person at the next table in a night-restaurant is French. Apart from the tall country carts which bring turnips and carrots, beautifully washed, and arranged in gold and silver ramparts, into the town at darkest midnight and early dawn, there are hay-carts, as sweet as morning, trundling sleepily among the afternoon noise and clang of traffic. In a street leading from a tram-ridden artery a man in an earth-coloured blouse stands upon a golden pile of straw as high as a little Arc de Triomphe, and pitchforks it methodically into one of the many 'gréniers d'abondance' still existing above Paris houses, each with its mansard window and its rusty iron pulley.

The villages of Paris are scattered all over its area. There is one near the Roman arena, where the streets are named after naturalists, and the air is laden with barrel-trundlings from the wine market, and voices of the sorry wild beasts of the Jardin des Plantes. Passy and Auteuil are still villages; the Place d'Anvers, off the turbulent and shabby Boulevard Rochechouart, has some air of a village green; and even the Square du Temple, whose soil is fathoms deep in tragedy, sees every day a peaceful population, that might as well be native to the country places of a hundred miles away as to this dark cell of the great city's history, sitting round the weeping willow that commemorates the tower of sorrow. The Ile St. Louis is a tiny town in itself; its main street might be a hundred miles from anything bigger than some dependent hamlets. The Place des Fêtes at Belleville, the workmen's quarter, is as typical a village green as though no one had ever heard of cities, let alone of Labour Troubles, Class Warfare, and the rest.

Up in Montmartre there is an untouched village square. Not a slate, not a wall, has been altered in the Place du Tertre. Many have been obscured behind paper and calico advertisements of this picture-shop or that restaurant, but the houses are the same as they were decades and generations ago. At luncheon-time, and more especially

LA PLACE DU TERTRE
"An untouched village square"

at the dinner-hour on fine warm days, the entire square and its en-
virons are hidden beneath tables surrounded by tourists, mostly from
America, who are delighted to feel that they are being very Bohemian and unexacting because they accept a menu that offers but
little choice. As it always includes hot lobster and roast chicken, they
hardly have a right to reckon themselves among the shipwrecked or
the besieged, and they are far from considering themselves intruders.
Yet intruders they are.

Montmartre fourteen years ago (not the gay-Paree Montmartre,
but the quiet village upon the hill) knew nothing of the horrors of
war, and still less of the horrors of peace. It was still living to itself, as
any self-respecting community does. The people who came up to
dine on stifling nights outside the little tiled 'Coucou' fed by the
light of a fading sky and a great star. Presently a little oil-lamp was
brought out to each table, just when in neighbouring houses candles
shifted from window to window as protesting children were taken
from supper-table to bed. A cool wind blew, and an apple tree in
the sloping garden over the wall caught and lost and caught the star
in its slow old arms.

The service was leisurely, but nobody minded. At long last one
went and fetched one's food if one was impatient. But it was not a
place for the impatient. The waits were beguiled by the antics of
such children as were just too old to have been put to bed when the
little lamps were brought out (the local bed-tide-table). They
swarmed up and down a lamp-post at the corner, that looked like a
marshmallow, or vanished from sight abruptly down the balustrade
of the steep stairway that leads to baking Paris below; they wound
their legs round their necks and looked from between with cheerful
grins, giving one a feeling that the spaghetti one had just absorbed
had gone curly; they watched the eating, the love-making, and the
table manners of the diners with the utter unconcern of those who
have never had too much to eat, are too young to make love, and do
not care one depreciated centime whether you hit, embrace, or
address as 'Monsieur' the host of the evening.

Unexpected things happened, unheard of in villages, or even in
cities, but well known to dreams. Once, on a summer evening so

languid that it had dropped its amethyst gauze veil to the very earth, the diners and the children and the villagers heard a strange swinging clash, and through the violet dusk under the marshmallow lamp came tramping two Roman generals in armour, their helmets bravely plumed, their short swords sturdy at their sides. With them ran laughing loose-haired girls, as lightly-clad as the night, in floating wisps of rose and turquoise. Before the earth-coloured wall they passed, their shadows no more unbelievable than they, and stepped down into the dark stairway that leads to Paris, whose walls sent up echoes of their descent. On these slopes many such Romans fell, and many an Aspasia may have haunted their thoughts as they marched down to the standards of Rome arrayed against the barbarian; but they are unexpected among the trousers and tweeds of to-day. These were students going to the Quatz' Arts Ball, children at play, achieving, as children sometimes do, a magic-lantern presentation of truth in that evening air, while round eyes gazed upon them over the steaming dishes and the glow-worm lamps.

Nowadays, those little lamps are gone, and if you look up for the star you are stared out of countenance by an intermediate electric bulb. The fire-swallower, and the old musician with a bald head and a half-dead mandoline, plying their trade for halfpence in a furtive manner, and vanishing like shadows when a policeman's silhouette was flung forward by a kindly warning lamp – they have gone too. Their place has been taken by a fourth-rate revue of sad old singers and fiddlers; unsuccessful artists whose efforts at quick portraiture out-Herod the passport photographer; and tired, tired old ladies, quavering the songs of old unhappy far-off loves and kisses long ago, or working their thin fingers to the bone – not very far to go – on loud new pianos in loud new tunes that know nothing of the Mechlin and Mendelssohn of their laughing days. The surrounding houses echo to these strident pianos, or to jazz trios, and from far and near come neat young men in evening dress, trying to persuade you that if you will only come inside you will see something or hear something just naughty enough to please you, but not so naughty as to offend your wife.

But at ten o'clock in the morning, like wakening after nightmare, here is the village which in 1914 still talked, as if it were Tooting Bec, of the peril for one of its daughters in marrying one of 'these Parisians.' It was then preserving its life against the invading forces of tourists coming to see the sunrise on the one hand, and Apaches, or people looking for Apaches, on the other. The Montmartrois, after his long day's work, grumbled in his bed at all three, because they broke his well-earned rest. Heaven help the honest labouring man, how little he foresaw these Anglo-saxophone voices of the night!

In the morning the acacias whisper round the Place du Tertre, and the local children, who know the world, the flesh, and the devil when these come up 'the Hill' to dinner, settle down to marbles and pebble-games. On this spot the lion-hearted young mayor of Montmartre flung himself into the struggle of 1871. To this little peaceful square, now besieged by the self-conscious gaieties of the artists' 'Commune of Montmartre' and the liqueur-ridden dinners of the tourist, must often have turned during the Great War the thoughts of old Georges Clemenceau, that young mayor. He knew these walls, shabby and cracked, these plucky acacias; he knew the ancient church, its forgotten Merovingian cemetery, the windmills, the steep slopes, the Paris that growled at their feet; he knew every baby that played in the square, because he was the village doctor, and could tell whether peppermint or calomel was wanted when the mayoral windows admitted a captious cry; he knew everything except the crowds and the electricity, and the great white pile of the expiatory basilica close by. They came after.

In Montmartre village there is a lane ten minutes – perpendicular minutes – from a bus terminus, where an old door sagging on its hinges shows you the straight cottage-path, between cabbages and hollyhocks and a wild-branched rose-tree, leading up from two lilacs to the subsiding old farm-house. Once, while a passer-by stood looking, from a chamber above came the richness of a 'cello and the sweetness of a flute and a violin. It almost seemed that Time had grown younger, and in this remote country corner the last new work of this wonderful young W. A. Mozart was being tried, to see if it was good. It was, so they began again. 'And then the sounds of beauty flowed and trembled, and seemed, for a little space, to triumph over the pains of living and the hard hearts of men.'

In the morning the village squares of Paris are very much alive. The wives are doing their shopping, and, whether her husband has rolled off in a tram to his field and his barn, or burrowed into a roaring train on his way to a be-telephoned office where the typewriters clack all day, Madame has one and the same notion. A Frenchwoman may be married to a smock or a black coat, but her motto is: The most of the best for her sous. No wonder the Paris tradesman makes what he can of the foreigners – they are like a rest-cure to him, with their absurd habit of believing what he says and paying what he asks. And then, what a joke he has with which to sweeten the harder bargains! 'Ah, Madame Durand, you should have seen the English lady just now! Of course, the butter was good, because I don't sell bad butter, but do you think she knew or cared whether it was twenty or thirty centimes more a pound? Ah, they don't breed housewives like you, Madame Durand! And then, of course, with their cursed high exchange, they are rudely rich, all of them!'

Madame Durand, her basket on her arm, swallows the flattery, nods to the criticism, and with undeviating concentration proceeds to select the largest eggs.

She has a powerful ally in her daily struggle with the producer-cum-middleman price. There is no middle-class district in Paris which has not its weekly, bi-weekly, or daily open-air mart. Within a few paces of the haughtiest shop in the Avenue de l'Opéra is a covered market-place which differs only in the variety and quantity of its merchandise from that of Vieilleville-sous-l'Oubli. Many a bright and beautiful young British subaltern measured his length upon the casual cabbage leaves of the Marché Saint-Honoré when the Army's Assistant-Provost-Marshal reigned in a rickety tall house there, where the smell of apples and fish floated through the windows against a barrage of Virginian tobacco. Many a general blew testily from within his collar when beef and mutton, uncooked, assailed him on a hot day through his nice commanding nose. Many an officer, old enough to have avoided the trouble, wished to Heaven that the way from an all-night bridge party to the leave train did not lie quite so near quite so much food.

Immediately behind the Madeleine lies another of the unexpected markets of Paris. They are, indeed, scattered all over the city; but even more typical are those of the streets. The barrow-markets of London are not nearly so numerous as those of Paris, and are confined almost entirely to very poor thoroughfares. Here they are to be found in nearly all quarters. They represent a useful check upon the prices of the neighbouring shops, and they provide a delightful topic of conversation for the housewives of the city in the afternoon as they sit sewing in the nearest open space, on benches or inadequate-looking camp-stools.

A bargain in carrots, at a stall only twenty yards beyond the one where a neighbour let herself be diddled of a sou, is a merry subject for a third housewife, who is hugging herself because the Brie she found is so creamy, or the fish so fresh. Then there are the habits of other housewives to discuss: how So-and-So leaves everything to her cook, and never checks the accounts; and Such-and-Such comes marketing herself, with her servant behind her, and notes every price, so that the poor girl cannot get her sou in the franc; how Which-and-What stints his wife, so that she has to buy old potatoes instead of new; and how little Madame This-and-That prefers the ribbon and lace stalls to those where the calico and curtains are – for drapery, hosiery, haberdashery and foot-gearery are represented in most street markets and all village markets in France. In the immense roar of Paris, it is the classic clack of the market-place and the village square which occupies the placid and competent housewives in their little pools of peace, which fills their little local newspapers, and enlivens the *entr'actes* at the crowded cinema and the village theatre, where barn-storming is still in vogue, although one may sometimes hear good plays well done in local theatres, by casts that know their work even if their names are unknown.

The principal centre of a village, setting aside the church, is its general shop. There all the needs and most of the pleasures of the community are catered for; there the hard-earned wage and the iridescent pocket-money are spent; and the spenders make of the place a hot-bed of news which shames Reuter and the Associated Press, and any other agency ever yet heard of whose business was the collecting and dissemination of information.

115

There is hardly a street running from any spot of centralized traffic, even in the busiest heart of Paris, which has not its village shop. Sometimes it wears the brown countenance of a grocery; sometimes it is pale and rich, and an English visitor would call it a dairy. But it offers the most unlikely wares. The grocery has a counter for cooked vegetables, and the dairy deals in salads, and sells chocolate and rice and potatoes and fruit. Or the shop may be a greengrocery to all appearance, and yet provide milk, and butter, and beer, and macaroni, and eggs and flour. At these general shops one can buy every ingredient necessary for a long meal, except fish and meat, and even those are occasionally to be had, in the shape of smoked herrings or a rabbit.

They can really be called village shops, and their claim is clinched by the sweets they sell. A low board is fixed outside, and great glass jars are placed upon it, full of endless varieties of boiled sweets. The infant villagers cannot find bull's-eyes among them, but a gentler compound of peppermint and honey is sold, in the form of a flat, hard slab, twisted up in brightly-hued paper, and having a stick three inches long protruding from it as a handle; thus consecrating, if not rendering sanitary, the age-long custom, condemned by sterner countries, of taking the sweet out of the mouth to see if it has changed colour. There are jars of clear pink sweets, of cloudy yellow ones, of mixed drops with violently acid taste; jars containing all the pebbles of the seashore imitated in sugar; others full of solidified honey like solidified sunshine. In a country grocery of this nature, sixty yards from the Opéra, you can buy 'pork and green peas' — green sugar-balls interspersed with striped cubes to represent dice of bacon. Could any merchandise speak less of the thundering town and more of the quiet country — where people have time to suck sweets?

There are sweetshops in Paris whose very names might, and do, make mouths water on the Five Continents and (weather permitting) on the Seven Seas. They are wonderful places, dealing in chocolates of a sublimated description, in which the astral body of a nut is mingled with the spiritual effluescence of a bean under the superintendence of a fairy, or having the very soul of a liqueur imprisoned in frail walls of sweet brown. These shops also sell almonds firmly

116

"They can really be called village shops"

bound in hard sugar, the traditional dragées of every French christening; though why a toothless child should be given anything so hard as a sugar-plum it is difficult to say.

Marrons glacés and preserved fruits are found in these haughty emporia, and their shop-windows are quite like little exhibitions of decorative art, with their china bowls and figures, papier-maché and cardboard boxes, hollow dolls, fantastic baskets, and eccentric porcelain animals. They also abound in groves of that ribbon of which crops are grown in France especially for presents – it would be rude, almost indecent, to give anybody a plant or a bouquet or a pound of sweets without having it tied up with loops and bows like a pantomime poodle. So much associated with the idea of festivity are these super-bows of semi-silk that cases have been known of people fixing them to piano-backs, mantel-mirrors (the beloved *glaces dorées* of French landlords), screens, and curtains, where they catch the dust very nicely and competently, and suggest with equal force the pleasure of merriment and the usefulness of refuse-bins.

Even in the lesser sweetshops there are plenty of bows, so that at Easter-time a yellow fledgling breaking from a chocolate egg is sure to be adorned with neat-fingered ribboning, reflecting great credit on the foresight of the responsible hen.

But sugar has always been dear in France, and the sweetshops of Edgware Road and Charing Cross Road are unknown to Paris. Here the sale of sweets is usually combined with that of cakes or wines and liqueurs; and even such little shops as confine themselves to bonbons have never heard of any such things as Lansdowne Mixture or peppermint cushions or mint lumps, any more than of 'cokernut chunks', 'toasted squares,' or pineapple fingers. Even the fondant, in spite of its French name, is unknown to the Paris child; and hardbake or almond rock has ever been one of our island privileges. The only hardbake known to this city is sold, together with other beautifully made sweets, by an Italian dressed as cleanly as a barman; and he only appears in Montparnasse at so late a dinner-time that even the French child has gone to bed, and all the villages of Paris, save Montmartre, are beginning to darken down to themselves, like birds sinking into their feathers, oblivious of the metropolitan glare and roar about them.

The country is everywhere at hand in Paris, which has rural surprises for the observer. Up till a year or two before the War, a goatherd from Auvergne, in a country smock, piped his flock down the Rue des Martyrs every morning, so that all who wished could have fresh goats' milk. His goats were known by name, and one could call upon 'Anna' or 'Josephine' to be the regular provider of one's breakfast. The bleating mingled oddly with the noise of omnibuses groaning up the steep hill or dashing down it. Some districts still enjoy this daily visit of Pan. Again, every morning there is a sweet chinking music in the streets; it has that effect of clearness, and yet distance, which recalls cattle-bells heard from an opposite mountain-slope. It comes from the milk-woman, a load of full bottles in her weighted right hand, and a dozen or so of empty ones slung by their wire handles from her left, that tinkle together as if life were great fun, and a new day a great gift.

In Neuilly, no farther from the Opéra than is Hammersmith from Piccadilly Circus, one is perhaps engaged in deep wonder as to what a partner would do if taken out into spades, when suddenly a vision of the South Downs, complete with flocks and shepherds and a gleam of sun on the far floor of the Channel, entirely fills the mind. No effort of concentration can rout it; indeed, it grows stronger, for the barking of a collie is now quite distinct, and the carpet begins to feel like turf. 'There are those sheep again!' says the hostess. 'They drive them past here every evening.' She adds, raising her voice a little because of a couple of trams putting the brake on near by, 'It's really dreadful how noisy sheep can be.'

Overlooking the yard of Saint-Lazare railway station, where rich travellers with their jewel-cases roll across the stones in silent cars on their way to or from New York and London, a large selection of sabots is on sale. Some are all of wood, some have leather uppers; the wooden soles are nearly an inch thick, and are eloquent of village paving and country mud, of single windows shining through wet dusk across the fields, of tired men talking by the fire in little inns; but if they could move forward across the road, ten yards would land them among the wardrobe trunks and the neat American feet shod in fur-soft leather. That is Paris all over.

118

and the Rue du Vaugirard in the evening

Human beings all need warmth, light, sleep, food and drink, and one of the wonders of the world is the infinite ingenuity with which humanity has enclosed these necessities in huge walls of custom, and erected into a matter of difficulty and of difference, sometimes of serious quarrel between individual, clan, or nation, the fashion of their enjoyment.

On a very clear day one can sit on the cliffs by Dover with eyes on school-children going into their homes in France, and ears full of English children clattering into their cottages just behind. They have all been learning lessons, they are all hungry for a meal, and presently they will all be put to bed. Their necessities are the same, but the likeness ends there. The very print in each school-book is odd to that other child across the water; the knapsacks are totally different; the bread and the butter are other in shape and size and colour and taste; the tea and the soup would be mutually unwelcome; and although there are blankets and sheets upon both beds, they are differently woven and disposed, the very pillows have diverse forms, and the beds stand upon floorings as far apart in idea as red tiles and jute. Yet with a motor-boat one could attend the two suppers on the same day; tuck up the English child at sunset and the French one by twilight; and be startled by the likeness of one little bullet head upon a pillow to another, the moment that slumber has obliterated those queer walls of speech and habit that we build between ourselves and others in our waking moments.

The outstanding differences between French and English homes are in the attitude towards physical comfort and hospitality. No well-bred French person ever lolls; the arm-chair of the bourgeois by his dining-room fire and the stately bergère of the marquise in her Aubusson salon alike have straight backs and rigid arms. In a typical French drawing-room there is a horseshoe of little chairs, closed by two bergères and the fireplace at one end, and having a settee at the top. On these the company sits and converses with remarkable ease, considering how difficult it is to be natural and fluent when the whole circumstances suggest that one is expected to be as witty as Beaumarchais and as mannered as Marivaux. Private conversations are not allowed, either at table or in this charmed circle;

the talk must be kept general, and any interludes between neighbours or *vis-à-vis* must not be more than three remarks long.

In the smoking-room the chairs are more comfortable, but not nearly so yielding as they would be in England. Really downy seats and couches are only to be seen in the windows of shops devoted to the most modern of decorative art; on the stage, in scenes where the hero is liable to wear a blue velvet coat embroidered in gold, and is certain to be awaiting the visit of a lady; or in actual flats belonging to these luxurious members of society, or to ladies who live behind orange curtains and under pink lamps. The normal French family has as little truck with such enervating softnesses as the heartiest English squire accepts and likes, when he and his pipe sink into the sympathetic leather, and commune with the fire about the hardness of to-day's run and the nasty cropper the poor old vicar came at High Hanger, as it has with anything so violent as fox-hunting.

In wealthy Paris flats the notions of Versailles in its great days can be seen, compressed, but complete. There is no room for them, and this leads often to a congestion of furniture; but the underlying idea is integrally there. Life is a brilliant and social affair, and requires a certain formality which will enable it to be run on brilliant and social lines; powerful emotions and appetites should be kept in the attic, or at least dressed in silk and velvet and taught how to behave before they are allowed to appear in the drawing-room. One is never so tired as to wish to lean back (if one is, one should go to bed); one is never so sad that an epigram and a bout of smiling talk should not be a perfect cure (if one is, one should have gone to church); one is never too old to be witty and interesting (if one is, one should have gone to the churchyard); and one is never, never, never both plain and dull (or, in Heaven's name, why did one not dash to a nunnery, or a monastery, the day one was born, and show that at any rate one was not also mentally defective?).

Those are the ideas underlying the rich furniture of France; the ideas which Louis the Great so firmly impressed upon his country's consciousness that, so soon as a French family can afford them, it buys ancient or modern bow-legged gilt chairs, palely tapestried, delicate carpets, gilt console-tables, and crystal chandeliers. These things have even come to be a sort of domestic patent of good-breeding; if one was brought up with them, and/or inherited them and the ways that go with them, the supposition is that one is of good family. It is not a question of money, because solid modern furniture costs quite as much as good copies or dilapidated specimens of fine old stuff. It is not even a question of taste, because a person of no taste might as easily be captured by bad modern Louis XV, with its blatant gold and its coarse fabric, as by over-varnished, half-seasoned walnut. It is a question of habits of living; and not even the Revolution has altered the French conviction that real politeness and real brilliancé are somehow supported by household furnishings which belong, either in truth or by imitation, to the period which first made those qualities famous.

French furniture of lesser standing has a very different idea behind it. Thrift is the first virtue in every ordinary household, and that things should be solid, and last long, and not show the dirt, and not need outlay or upkeep — this is what is demanded of them. Like Mrs. Primrose, they are selected for such qualities as will wear well. Obviously eighteenth-century brocade had that virtue, since we still enjoy a great deal of it; but its modern copy is not so reliable, and the middle-class Paris family only agrees with the practical, efficient provinces, in preferring rep, corduroy and neutral-hued tapestry for its upholstery.

In the matter of house-linen, no German woman could dwell more lovingly on the thought of her cupboard than does the average Frenchwoman. They would both agree cordially that the English-woman is culpably careless, uses her beautiful table-cloths with a recklessness that is really shocking, and has no better reason to give than that a table should be agreeable to look upon. As though that matters if the food be good! There are decent middle-class English families helping themselves to ruin in laundry bills to-day, just as though "American" cloth (Americanisé, oil-cloth; the "waxed cloth" of France) had never been invented; and it would be difficult to measure the relative disapproval of the British and the French house-wife in considering their respective desires: (*a*) to save the wear and tear and cost of laundry, and (*b*) to have the table delicately set, even if times are so hard that an egg or bread and cheese may be the only fare. In France a table is that surface on which meals are served; its possible decorative use is quite neglected by a large number of French families, corresponding in position to English households where the manner of serving food is a matter of real importance. French food is beautifully arranged upon the dishes after its ex-quisite cooking, but the dishes are often placed upon a table of very utilitarian countenance; unless, of course, there are guests.

It is, perhaps, upon the question of guests that the difference be-tween the Paris and the London home is most clearly marked. An Englishwoman coming to live in Paris has a tremendous tussle with her servants when they are told that the spare-room bed must be kept ready for unexpected use. There is hardly any impromptu hos-pitality in the French family, even in Paris; be the night never so wet, the bridge-guest will not expect to be offered a shakedown; be the unexpected meeting in the business quarter never so reminiscent of boyhood days, the host will say, 'What day next week or the week after can you come to dinner?' sooner than, 'Now you're for it, old chap; home you come to pot-luck and stay the night, or there'll be trouble.' Indeed, he is more likely to say, 'You must lunch with me one day,' and not invite the guest to his home.

Not only in Paris, but all over France, domestic life is organized with strict attention to the family habit of almost Oriental seclusion and a need for thrift.

A closed home appeals to the Frenchman. He likes to feel that the tide of his life flows gently and unbroken through the pool he has dug and fortified for himself; and he likes also to feel that if anything disturbs it, such as a proposed dinner-party, the resulting eddies and foamings will be proportionate to the occasion. Unlike the English-man, who, if signs of domestic hurry appear upon the horizon, will fly to any club whose telephone is guaranteed not to work, a French-man really admires his wife when she is in something of a carfuffle about a dinner-party. He watches her, indeed, with just the inter-ested awe which she shows for him when he has directors in town, or a board meeting on hand, or something of the kind.

Neither he nor she has the least glimmering of a feeling that anything pretentious could be found in this notion of hospitality. The more trouble the hostess takes, the greater the compliment to the guests; and it follows that the compliment should be visible to the guests, and that they should be visibly sensible of it. Hence a French dinner-party will, does, and should, include conversation appreciative of the effort made. There is not a hostess in England, of the class which is personally, however augustly, in touch with the housekeeping, the menu, and the service, who could resist an apparently spontaneous remark that such a room, such a dish, or such a butler or parlour-maid is a marvel; but in France open admiration for all that has to do with the house that is offering hospitality is accepted and expected.

During the War we had a British propaganda in France — so it was said, at least; and those who knew the Britons engaged in it in Paris remember well how hard they worked, and how difficult it was for them to overcome the obstacles they had to meet. For instance, an authority on statuary sent them articles on the British policy in Cyprus for insertion in Paris newspapers. The Paris newspapers about then — 1917 — were rather full of other matter, for a good deal was going on; and these articles were lost in the diabolic thunder of guns on the front, the infernal symphony of air-raids.

But nobody ever thought well, apparently, to try to explain to the two peoples even such differences as these in their domestic life:

(*a*) [important] One should be lyric in praise of a French entertainment, to an extent which would sound insincere to an English hostess; and,

(*b*) [cardinal] On meeting a French friend who has lost a relative, however close, one should immediately express all one's regret and sympathy, adding a testimony to the fine qualities of the departed; and should not be embarrassed if this very naturally makes the friend, even if a man, cry.

French people think one colder than an iceberg if one does not do this. How many friendships between 1914 and 1926 may not have frozen into silence, and subsequently into dislike, because nobody ever explained that the British do the extreme opposite of the French in this respect? If one puts this particular case to a French friend, even if that friend have a large English acquaintance, it is a hundred to one that this difference of hearth-custom has never been definitely understood; the odds are that after thought the French friend will add: 'Then *that* was why Jones never — I see!' or words to that effect. Add the other side to it, explaining that you could not be harder on an English citizen with a whip than with verbal condolences on a raw sorrow, and an appalled glance will be the answer, with that rare blush which upon the colourless Latin skin means real embarrassment, as your interlocutor casts back to things said with the kindest intentions. Nobody in war-time told the two principal combatants any of these things; nobody in peace-time thinks of them; and the two countries continue to flounder in misunderstanding of those details of behaviour which make up the sum of everyday life to those who wish to live together in amity.

Happy life together consists in knowing each other's ways and likings, and establishing a sliding-scale of give and take which will result in a comfortable fireside. Neither in the big things which sometimes matter (as in the case of war, burglars, fire, love and volcanoes), nor in the little ones which always do (such as baths, breakfast, morning, luncheon, afternoon, tea, evening, dinner, billiards, bridge, conversation, dancing and bed), does the average Englishman or Frenchman ever get a really good road-map that he can follow in the other chap's country.

Hence the Englishman does not always do his duty at a French meal, which will not matter once he realizes it, because then he can apologize and all will be forgiven, if the apology or its wording be lame; but will matter a good deal if his French language is better than his French manners, because then it will be argued that if he can pronounce French like that he ought to know what French to pronounce. This may be a fallacy, but fallacies can be very important. This is certain: it is almost impossible for a foreigner to be conversant with the ins and outs of French family life to such an extent that a foreign accent can be discarded; speak like a Frenchman, and you will be expected to act like one. The position is logical. (The danger threatens but few foreigners.)

124

Moreover, speaking like a Frenchman, you will also be expected to hand plates like one. Even in broken French this is required. This is a very complicated business; at moments it becomes like cat's-cradle, when full plates and empty are being rapidly exchanged between the host and his farthest guests. (They are quite a long way off, because he and his wife sit nose to nose across the equator of the table, leaving most of the guests in polar darkness north and south. The Veneerings did it too.)

In France no guest's place should ever be left without a plate. If there is going to be a wait between courses, which frequently happens (because eating is a serious matter here, and not one to be galloped), a plate is put before every one, lest an awful moment arrive when it occur to somebody that a piece of French lace or linen or Chinese embroidery is a poor substitute for food. Therefore, in private houses and in restaurants, plates are put before you to keep your mind quiet, even if they are quite cold and the dish to come is hot; in the latter case they will be changed at the last moment. In houses where there are sufficient servants this will be done by them; otherwise the cat's-cradle begins, and the host exchanges laden hot plates for empty cold ones. With no extra help in the kitchen to wash up between-whiles, it must need at least eighty-four plates to give twelve people five courses at a Paris table. And there are usually at least six courses.

In even quiet households this disposition of plates exists. The head of the household may have to serve soup to four people; each place will have a plate, and the full one will be handed out by the server's right hand while his left has to be stretched forth to receive the empty one. To pile all four before the server would be quite shocking to French notions; it would mean that three people passed a period ranging from fifty seconds to two minutes with no plates before them, and that would be a dreary and inhospitable series of moments.

One cannot too soon learn and accept the axiom that when one is at table in France, food is the business in hand, and nothing else. It is certainly good enough to be, and obviously the English are wrong in wanting table-cloths and flowers when the dominant affair of the moment is food and plates.

As to notions of fish-knives, they belong to the wealthy and cosmopolitan classes. Elsewhere it is known that a steel knife will cut a fish as neatly as anything else. Moreover, there may be three plates where one would do, but one knife and fork must suffice, in many a French household with pretensions to gentility, for the three or four courses between the fish and the cheese (which comes before the sweet).

If knives are scarce, napkins are lavish, being usually more like young sheets than the enlarged handkerchiefs which serve in England. They began in France during the fifteenth century, in the guise of bibs for children. Erasmus decided a hundred years or so later that, since adults had adopted this fashion, the napkin should be worn either across the shoulder or the left arm. This moderate counsel was later overridden by citizens wearing ever more elaborate costumes, and anxious to safeguard them, who tried to knot their napkins behind their well-fed necks, thus in fact, inaugurating a phrase nowadays associated with anything but plenitude of food; they 'tried to make the two ends meet.' But it began at a time when knives were so few that the Swiss habit of carrying each his own was as much laughed at as monocles are to-day in New York, and it was a fashionable fad among the ultra-rich to place upon their tables ebony-handled knives (two or three for a tableful) in Lent, and ivory handles for the rest of the year.

There is a belief prevalent among the French servants employed by British residents in Paris that 'the English eat a great deal.' After a month or so these servants change their opinions; they have discovered that a couple of well-cooked dishes, plus cheese amply suffice the Anglo-Saxon employer when alone; that a third course meets the case when there are but four or five at table; and that even a state meal of nine or ten is not to consist of endless apparitions of rich food, but of a logical sequence of simple flavours. In cosmopolitan circles, where the chef is mightier than the hostess, this moderation is as little the case as in the small suburban flat, where the hostess is the cook, and glories in it, as she has every right to do.

In a kitchen 6 feet by 8 feet, with a charwoman's help or without it, the bourgeoise of Paris will achieve marvels which seem to have demanded an equipment like the annual Gas Show, and a staff fit for the Café de Paris. Everything is beautifully cooked, beautifully displayed, and the courses, like the poet's days, 'se suivent et ne se ressemblent pas,' unless the house-pride of the hostess has misled her into too many sauces. Knowing the size of the kitchen, one can drop into wonder, as in the presence of magic, when the endless succession of dishes continues to appear, like the bowls of jewels on the heads of Aladdin's slaves, from the little room with the double gas-ring and the wee oven underneath.

The hostess herself may be a little flushed, but never unbecomingly; for the good reason that the flush produced by the efficient preparation of good food is by association of ideas a beauty in her eyes and those of her guests. One of the reasons why an Englishman remains a barbarian in the French idea is his habit of looking upon food as a necessity rather than a pleasure; there is a dark suspicion that he is on occasion so benighted as to consider that necessity a nuisance! (Hence, of course, the well-known horrors of the English table – cold roast beef, nearly raw, eaten with Worcester sauce and watery potatoes, in a fireless room with the window open and the year-long fog of England outside. Oh, là, là!)

American visitors, fresh from their own servant problem, ought to be deeply in sympathy with the housewife of France. They would be if they were not even more deeply horrified by her kitchen. Fresh from white tiles, glass vessels, constant hot water, ice chests and cabinet cupboards, the American woman looks with pity and terror upon the dark cubby-hole which plays the part of kitchen in the average middle-class Paris flat. It has brought inconvenience to a high art; no smallest opportunity of wasting space has been forgotten; and if it has been found possible to place the larder facing due south, while excluding air and sun from the kitchen itself, this has been done with a dexterity that cannot be too highly rated. There are things about Paris kitchens which can only be explained on the supposition that the devil is afraid of happy home life, and sees to it that architects shall work against it. Why else should a kitchen, unusually large, having an area of about 12 feet by 8, be built over by a range of about 6 feet by 3, out of which the grate itself has a paltry diameter of 8 inches? This great steppe of iron, filled with big iron cupboards, in the depths of which dirty rags and the lost silver teaspoon (in halves) and a mummied mouse are occasionally found, is moreover fitted with an enormous mediaeval chimney, so nicely proportioned that only one narrow shelf can run round it outside, while no cook taller than 5 feet 7 inches can hope to escape contracting a permanently bumped skull in her leanings and withdrawals about her pans.

French servants are better than English ones and do more. They can all sew, and are expected to do the household mending. They can all cook, and English Sunday supper is unknown, because when the cook is out the housemaid does the cooking; and as she detests cold meat, she does it willingly – ham and galantine are the only cold meats acceptable to French palates. They are of a much higher state of education and civilization than any English servants, save those of the butler-housekeeper class, which is to the rest of domestics in England what the Brahmins are to other castes in India. No friendliness on the part of a mistress, though it will be greatly appreciated, will lead to offensive familiarity on the part of French servants. They often have remarkable philosophies which are well worth listening to. Thus, one Normandy cook, finding herself the cause of annoyance to her mistress because she had thrown away some valuable china that could have been mended, remarked: 'Madame mustn't "make herself any bad blood" about this, because that is dreadfully tiring, especially in this heat, and Madame doesn't like being angry; and after all, I thought Madame would never know the things had been broken if I threw them away, so then she would have been spared all annoyance. Now if I had *meant* to annoy Madame –' By the time Madame had found her way through this tangle of cajolery, sophistry, cunning, solicitude and common sense, there seemed nothing for it but a shrug and an indulgence in our national monosyllable. Thus does philosophy breed philosophy.

Many Paris servants over 20 (they are nearly always provincials – like most other Parisians) have at least one baby boarded out in the country, being kept by its mother; for although the law does now allow a woman to sue her child's father for its maintenance, in practice she seldom does so. A system of herding all the servants in a house on the top floor, in a series of cold, dark cubicles, has a better effect upon the country's birth-rate than upon its morals. Once out of the flat where he or she works, the Paris servant expects to be at complete liberty, and the kindliest supervision by the mistress, even though directed entirely toward the welfare of the servant, will be resented. This independence between 9.30 p.m. and 7 a.m., plus the system of top-floor cells which has nothing of the monastic save a complete lack of physical comfort, is largely responsible for the fact that so many female servants in Paris have growing babies learning to love foster-mothers in the country. There is no more devoted father in the world than the married Frenchman; but the mother-instinct of the Frenchwoman is so highly esteemed, and so much to be depended on, and a young man's essays in romance are so tolerantly regarded, that motherhood among servants is a common condition.

These are the girls of the unsheltered class among the respectable small bourgeois. They leave home, and thereby gain a liberty rigorously denied to any daughter of the aristocracy or the mediocracy whose parents have the money to keep her at home. (It may be added that in these disintegrating days the parents also need force of character — but that is another problem.) The domestic servant is launched upon a world where her official outings may be restricted to four hours on one afternoon a week, but where she is to be completely independent at night. She does not want to have her room actually in the flat of her employer; she wants the general independence of the horrid little top-floor room, even when it is unheated and unlighted. She needs much persuasion to 'live in,' in the English sense.

She certainly has a right to dispose of her leisure as she chooses, if good work can give it her. She cleans, sews, cooks, telephones, runs messages, with commendable good-will. She needs keeping up to her duties as often as an English maid, but has a larger view of them and, in most cases, greater competency. She is less given to the shibboleth of 'It's not my work' than is Mary Ann.

This is not to say, of course, that there is no servant problem in France. There is; but it depends less on scarcity of labour and competence than on expenses and the housing question. Most people have to live in smaller flats nowadays, many of which have no servant's room in the house; and although the same kind of maid who was paid Frs. 70 a month before the War now gets Frs. 375, which works out in sterling at very much the same amount, it is a terrific sum in francs to those who earn in francs. The employer's salary has not kept pace with the exchange value of the franc, and the price of all the thirteen basic necessities of life, which have to be provided for servants as for employers, has far outskipped it.

It may, and does, thus arise that a cook will ask for higher wages on the score that real silk stockings and lizard shoes are so expensive; while the mistress, weighted down by the price of the mutton, beef, gas, electricity, etc., consumed in the kitchen, has to be content with vegetable silk and dowdy kid.

French servants dress very well, and with good taste. On their days out they wear clothes quite as discreetly chosen as those of their mistresses; their best hat is never afflicted with the awful Best-hattishness of an English Sunday-outer. In hours of service, however, they have very distinct notions of their rights. The cap-and-apron standard of England, the morning print and afternoon black, are unknown to the ordinary little French household. There are few more astounded countenances than that of the newly-installed Englishwoman who sees her 'general' preparing to wait at table in a bright blue blouse, a string of coral, and a brown skirt, all very obvious behind the provided apron. French servants will wear the caps of their region, Brittany, Vendée, Auvergne; but never the caps of servitude, unless they belong to the Brahminical caste of domestic. In upper middle-class French houses they wear black to serve at table, but this is a concession.

Registry offices exist, but it is characteristic of French life that the usual way of getting servants is by inquiry through the tradespeople. This method has one advantage: no servant will offer to serve unless the place is well spoken of by a consensus of local opinion. Thus, the outgoing housemaid may have said most unflattering things to the dairywoman, who may, however, have heard better ones from the greengroceress through the cook; and as the tradespeople are mostly permanent in the neighbourhood, employers arrive in the course of time at the standing accorded them by this unofficial tribunal. It also follows that the servant thus found, presented, and accepted, enters the new place in possession of so much information about the employers that, like Anstey's astrologer, he or she could 'tell them much in their past lives of which they had hitherto been ignorant.' And that saves the servant from devoting the first fortnight to research work.

In the fifteen hundreds, 'It was already a subject of complaint that good servants were so rare. Nearly all cheated their employers. Also the women-servants were reproached with having lovers; and with retaliating to reproach by breaking something. "Without servants household goods would last for ever," says Olivier de Serres.' The sixteenth-century Paris quotation shows that in this case at any rate the Paris hearth is one with the hearths of many countries; and as for centuries, they are in this regard mere unhasting nothings!

By NIGHT, TWO CONFLAGRATIONS ARE REFLECTED IN THE PARIS sky in diffused patches of angry glow. Southward, the patch of red calls up a picture of miles of market-carts all neatly packed with trim virginal carrots and turnips; of giants grunting under hundred-weights of food. You can almost hear the shouting, and feel the pushing and jostling. The Northern Light, which is by far the stronger of the two, hangs over Montmartre as though a bit of Hell had been opened.

Foreign pessimists who see in the lady of the 'Vie Parisienne' a true type of Parisian womanhood, also regard Montmartre as being essentially Parisian and full of light-hearted Latin gaiety relieved every now and then by some melancholy tragedy of life. It is easy to dramatize night Montmartre; to talk of it as the home of the drug maniac, to see in every 'chasseur' a trafficker in 'snow,' 'coke,' and ether; to think of it as a place where those disappointed in life or in love seek feverishly to drown both in champagne and orchestral cacophony; to dwell upon its sordid sins, its perverted prostitutions, its criminals, its Apaches and bullies. They all exist at any rate in sufficient quantity, and so openly as to enable Anglo-American moralists to thank God that London and New York have no such flaring catherine-wheel of harlotry. Unfortunately for such Peck-sniffian laments upon the perversity of Parisians, not only are the professional frequenters of Montmartre largely foreigners, but the great majority of its customers is actually British or American. Indeed, during the height of the American tourist season, the Champagne zone is almost entirely occupied by those young Americans whose main idea of seeing Paris is to make a day round of the many fashionable American bars where they are almost guaranteed against contact with the foreigner, and to spend the night with Charleston and Champagne in the same exclusive society. This view-point is aptly put by the remark of a young College boy who bumped into an intrusive Frenchman: 'This'd be a fine city if there weren't so many foreigners about.' Curiously enough, that also expresses the senti-ments of a Parisian who, while for sound pocket-reasons welcoming the visitor, regrets that he does not sometimes remember some of the susceptibilities of the local tribesmen. The touristocrat has killed

133

Montmartre, and although to-day the facilities offered to a young fool to make a bigger fool of himself are more than in the past, they have none of the old leaven of wit. Old Montmartre is dead. Young devils who sang while they starved, wrote verse to amuse themselves without a thought of publisher, daubed out 'croûtes' while munching a crust; men such as Maurice Donnay, Forain, Verlaine, Willette, Catulle Mendès and Degas, have passed on to fame, and there is none to take their place. Now, all that Montmartre produces, apart from headaches and police-court cases, is fat bank-balances for champagne profiteers. Instead of Pierrot's 'Clair de Lune' there is the angry reflection of a thousand sky-signs. Dead indeed is Pierrot's candle.

What the French, with their genius for maltreating a foreign tongue, call '*les dancings*' have replaced the old cabarets, for folk nowadays find more amusement in the antics of their own feet than in the wit of other men's brains. The old cabarets grew out of a café's clientèle or an artist's studio. Now the 'dancings' and music-halls spring Minerva-like, armed with jazz-bands and lounge-lizards, from the brains of company-promoters. Instead of the intimate personal touch of such places as the 'Chat Noir' there is a 'Société Anonyme.' Instead of characters such as La Goulue you have the Dolly Sisters. Anyone who hopefully thinks that he is going to catch some spirit of gaiety in Montmartre is reminded by constantly clicking cash registers that he is not a Bohemian bent upon enjoyment, but one of the world's workers earning a dividend for a joint stock company. That is the sole excuse for his presence, and in varying degrees the boy who opens the door, the cloak-room attendant, the girl who sells dolls, the flower-girl, wine-waiter, the girl you dance with, the barman, the waiter, the maître d'hôtel, the leader of the orchestra, the music-hawker and the *chasseur* impress this view of duty upon the customer.

By the time he has done the regular round, and closed the proceedings with onion soup, mussels or other of the traditional seven-o'clock-in-the-morning supper-dishes, he is quite certainly lighter in his pocket and heavier in his head than when he set out to see Paris night-life. If he has been to one of the *boîtes* most in fashion, he will indeed have seen typical Paris life. The proprietor is a Spaniard, the

134

LE MOULIN ROUGE
"Dead indeed is Pierrot's candle"

manager an Argentine, the American barman a Portuguese nigger. There is a coloured band for jazz music and an Argentine orchestra for the tango. One or two of the waiters may be French, the rest are Swiss or Italian. The few special turns performed during the night are usually given by knife-throwing Georgians, by Russian or Anglo-Saxon dancers. Among the guests there may occasionally be found a provincial 'nouveau-riche,' but Parisians are as rare as angels.

They are more frequently to be found in the less expensive establishments where champagne at three hundred francs a bottle is not obligatory; in music-halls such as the Moulin Rouge, where instead of the old *ombres* which made the fame of the Quatz' Arts, Mistinguett and the Dolly Sisters fight for the top of the bill, and the rest of the fare is provided by Anglo-American comedians and by swarms of girls whose nudity is held out as a bait to the tourist. After an evening spent in watching the manipulations of a Japanese conjurer, the flourishing legs of 'Les 16 Rosies Beauties' or 'Les 32 Fisher's Girls' and much parading and dressing and undressing of '250 pretty girls dressed in jewels and furs and feathers,' the foreign visitor to the modern successor of the Montmartre Cabaret goes away with a high idea of the sparkling wit of the French revue and exact notions as to the 'chic' of the Parisian artiste. Meanwhile Parisian members of the audience are engaged in wondering what sort of savages these Anglo-Saxons may be, who are ruining their city.

For while there are still one or two places in which with the right party you can have an enjoyable and sane evening in Montmartre, their number is become exceedingly small, and as a window upon any aspect of real Parisian life Montmartre might just as well be shuttered. Here again there is a curious difference between advertisement and fact. The whole world looks upon this Hill as an abode of Vice which, if not licensed by austere morality, becomes in some peculiar way more tolerable because it is in Montmartre. And it is undeniable that night-Montmartre represents none of the higher virtues and most of the lower vices. Yet it is there, giving a large-scale performance of *Box and Cox*, that inhabit some of the thriftiest and most sober working Parisians. They dwell there cheek by jowl with some of the world's worst rascals. Prostitutes and bullies, criminals and degenerates of every kind prowl through its streets and crowd its cafés at night. Black Maria, or the Salad Basket, as the French call that social dust-cart, goes off every morning to the depot with a full load of human refuse gathered overnight on the slopes of the Mount of Martyrs. No other quarter of Paris can equal its record of violent assault and murder. Nowhere is the police more certain of making a better criminal catch of women who have not observed regulations, of old lags who have broken the conditions of their tickets of leave, of 'wanted' criminals of every class, from the confidence trickster with his cigar and diamond shirt-studs to the Apache with his cap and muffler.

A visitor to Montmartre during the day-time would find considerable difficulty in identifying the dull drabness of the streets with the thoroughfares of flaming light he saw at night. Box has gone to bed, and Cox is abroad on his business. Poulbot's famous *gosses* are on their way to school. Women, not the silk-stockinged variety, are about in felt slippers or even clogs, with a yard or two of bread and a vegetable-filled string bag as their cargo. Everywhere there is the bustling noise made by thrifty hardworking people pursuing their trade or their craft. Generally speaking, the inhabitants of Montmartre are poor, for while as a residential district it has the advantage of height, it also has the drawbacks of narrow, noisy streets, many of which smell, not so much of drains as of the lack of them. It is a region of small crafts and trades, of one-man businesses. The few big stores cater for lean purses, for it is the dormitory of the poorly-paid clerk, typist, shop-assistant and sewing-girl who pour down to 'town' when sleepy-eyed waiters are just clearing up behind the last revellers.

Jazz and champagne are mainly confined to the foothills of Montmartre, but already the char-à-banc is carrying the tourist in noisy numbers to destroy the quiet peace of the summit, where like a ghostly pearl the dome of the Sacré Cœur floats above the city. The sinners have drunk themselves deeply in half-way up the Hill, but the saints and the martyrs remain in occupation at the top, where, indeed, Christianity in Paris had its birth.

There, Saint Denis, Saint Rustique, and Saint Eleuthère refused to bow in the temple to Mercury. Thence it was that Saint Denis went to heaven, bearing in his hands the offering of his decapitated head. It was in the underground galleries of the quarries which furnished the stone and plaster of Paris that the early Christians met in secret to escape persecution from the Roman occupier. There stands Saint-Pierre, one of the oldest churches in Paris. In the Martyrs' Chapel, Ignatius Loyola founded the Society of Jesus. The summit and the slopes were occupied by a vast Abbey of the Sisters of Saint-Denis, many of whose names are perpetuated in streets which now rock with the Charleston. The Abbess who was known as 'La Dame de Montmartre' would be somewhat surprised if she could see to-day those who have followed her.

The Order had its ups and downs. The ladies composing it, of whom one was Queen of France, farmed their estate where now the tramcar marks the only furrows that are cut with success. Along the heights arose that chain of windmills for grinding of wheat which became a distinguishing feature of Montmartre, and of which the Moulin de la Galette is now a dancing-hall with some title to be called Parisian. The last of the Abbesses, Madame de Mont-morency-Laval, when the storm of the Terror was dying down, joined the list of Montmartre martyrs. She was guillotined two days before the end of the Terror. She was seventy-one years of age and nearly blind, and was executed on the spot where, for the same faith, Saint Denis died fourteen centuries before.

The church of Saint-Pierre alone remains of the old Abbey. Revolutionary iconoclasm gave short shrift to its estates, which were sold, its cemetery, which was destroyed, and its shrines, which were pulled down. The furniture of the Abbey was auctioned off, its treasure of gold and silver carried to the Mint, while with the puerile grandeur that marks so much of the madness of those days, the iron and lead torn from the Abbey buildings were taken to the Arsenal, there to be forged into Revolutionary weapons against Church and State, in much the same spirit that rechristened the hill Mont Marat. With the same mean spite an anti-clerical municipal council in our day erected outside the Sacré Cœur a statue to a martyr in a different cause – the young Chevalier de la Barre, who for refusing to uncover to a religious procession was burnt alive. The statue commemorating the last man to be burnt by the Church was, with infinite tact, placed immediately under the statue of Christ which, in the attitude of benison, looks over the city. Fortunately, work which is still going on around the Sacré Cœur has given an opportunity of removing the Chevalier to a place of less prominence, where a more tolerant age may happily leave him.

The Commune saw the last of Montmartre's martyrs when Georges Clemenceau was mayor in a dingy two-storied house in the Place du Tertre. Rioting broke out over the disposition of the cannon dragged by turbulent Montmartre from the Champs-Elysées to the Butte, and despite young Clemenceau's efforts Generals Lécomte and Clement Thomas were done to death by the mob. That was the signal for the Commune.

A few, but very few, of the old traditions of Montmartre, whether political or artistic, still live. Poulbot remains true to the Hill and the little kids he has immortalized. Charles Neumont of the Humourists still has his studio hanging like a beetling crag over the city from the Place du Calvaire. There are still one or two real Montmartre cafés left, but the starving painter or poet who sought to-day to pay for his meal with a drawing or a song would in most cases very quickly find that the days of romance were over. Such things were possible right up to the outbreak of war. More than one poet or painter is alive to-day thanks to a café-keeper, who perhaps realized that the presence of an unmistakable group of Bohemians willing to improvise remarkably good verse and decorate the walls of the establishment with amusing frescoes attracted a larger and more profitable clientèle. In those days Bohemia was a land of incredible light and shade, of high spirits and desperate depression. Men who have travelled through it and have arrived in a country flowing with publishers' contracts and honour have confessed to the mingled emotions of nausea and regret aroused by memories of the days of their youth in Montmartre. When the 'Chat Noir' (which has vanished) and the 'Lapin Agile' (which still exists) were the home of an extraordinary versatile band of singing and painting youth, morbidity was all the fashion. The young fellows of those days did not all go as far as Peter Pan in thinking that 'to die would be a great adventure,' but they certainly felt that the starvation forced upon them by an inappreciative world of smug bourgeois was a necessary and maybe picturesque portion of their sacrifice upon the high altar of art. In the same sacred cause they had not only to scale the heights of ecstasy but also to plumb the depths of the most sordid cesspools of vice. They were in a way under the Byronic influence. Life in itself was not sufficiently strange for their tastes. Their lives had to be as disorderly and as mixed as their drinks and their drugs. They looked upon life anyhow as a rather poor jest played mainly at their expense. Before the war while many of them had come to a wretched finish some had won through to fame and comfort. During the war many confronted with 'The cream of the Jest' died smilingly ironic, with perhaps a regret that they could not make a song of their own ending. Some are now restaurant-keepers. There is even one of the old Montmartre brigade who runs a factory. Others have become successful either as playwrights, artists – even Picasso has convinced himself of the philosophy of his own pictorial jokes – or journalists, and there is hardly anyone left to carry on the tradition of the Hill as a Sanctuary for Singing-Birds and Engaging Lunatics.

An attempt has been made to revive the old fun of Montmartre, to give to it the note of Charpentier's 'Louise' by the institution of an Independent Republic of Montmartre. It arranges fêtes, pageants and feastings, but alas! Gaiety, like Truth, dies when it is organized. And the speculative builder is besieging the Hill. Already the spread of green slopes and fertile fields whereon the jolly millers of not so many years ago looked down to the north are covered with hideous sarcophagi of masonry replete with lifts, h. & c., electric light and 'tout le confort moderne.' Even the 'Lapin Agile' may find it difficult to escape, although the crown of the Hill still wears its village aspect, marred, however, by the all-pervading tourists' char-à-banc.

MONTPARNASSE, LIKE MONTMARTRE, IS MORE A MATTER OF MOOD than of geography, but, unlike Montmartre, it takes itself seriously, and with that sense of local patriotism so intensely developed throughout France, it affects to scorn dwellers on the Right Bank as being Philistines and bourgeois. Like Montmartre, Montparnasse has its night and its day life, its grave and its gay side, its foreign and Parisian aspect. The Latin Quarter, which formerly clustered round the Boule' Miche, the Luxembourg and the Sorbonne, has spread considerably of late years. It now is centred in Montparnasse, and, with the development of University Hostels at the Parc Montsouris, will be carried still farther away from its starting-point. The Boule' Miche is, however, still the main artery of student life. It is in that quarter that the remains of Bohemian gaiety are still sought, by lasses and lads more anxious to hie away to the Maypoles than to read the dry law or intestinal geography that shall later make of them Prime Ministers, world-famous scientists, or just dull, drab and disappointed village notaries or country doctors. Whereas Montmartre can only offer an incongruous picture of bald and blasé middle-age trying to kick its heels up like a colt, Montparnasse and the Boule' Miche have some of Youth's real friskiness. Fun on the Left Bank is, generally speaking, less alcoholic, and love is less commercial, than on the Northern height. While there a discussion on Allied War Debts might lead to a blow, in the Quarter it would take at least a difference of opinion over Picasso to start trouble. A French youth can work up a tremendous amount of enthusiasm on very little thin white wine. Even in youth, Parisians drink wine wisely and above all '*ils ont le vin gai.*' Their amusements are perhaps as puerile as those of the American College boys and 'men' at Oxford or Cambridge, and also much more precocious. The 'Varsity Rag, the Boat Race Night riot, the funeral of the undergraduate sent down are unknown, but the Parisian youngster has larks of his own equally futile and endearing to tolerant age. Chief among them is the '*Monome*' which, when it strays over to Right Bank boulevards, drives an already irate traffic-police completely off its head. A '*Monome*' is formed by two or three hundred students linking hands in single file. They career as wildly as possible through the main thoroughfares of the city, endeavouring all the time to keep the chain unbroken. When it is snapped there is a crazy rush to link it up again. Students as a rule thus disport themselves on their own side of the river, but on festive occasions such as *Mardi gras* and St. Catherine's Day they invade Right Bank Philistia, where they are warmly welcomed by merry midinettes and saucy shopgirls. Occasionally a '*Monome*' is made the medium of a political manifestation, and ends in a free fight with the police, but as a rule both police and public with a patient shrug and a kindly murmur of 'Ah, la jeunesse!' put up with whatever inconvenience it may cause.

This is about the only outlet the Paris student finds for his exuberance. While a good many of them have taken to football, tennis and other sports, there are no organized university or student games. Times are much harder than they were, and a student nowadays has not much time or money to devote to pleasure. He has to grind pretty closely for his degree, and many of them have to supplement their meagre allowance from home by tutoring, proof-reading, or some other part-time occupation. By far the most popular and by no means the least profitable of the jobs thus sought for by the student is that of cinema-super, for which he gets paid twenty francs a sitting. Poverty has robbed the Quarter of much of its jollity. There are only two cafés that can really be regarded as student haunts. Even student restaurants are rare, the high cost of living having forced students to meal with increasing assiduity in University House.

Hardly any painters are left in the old Quarter. They have emigrated, most of them, to Montparnasse, and a few farther afield to placid Passy. However artistic Montparnasse may be it does not provide a picturesque setting for Bohemianism. It is a region of tramcars, railways, and ham and beef shops. Its general squalor is almost relieved by the ugly modernity of the Boulevards Montparnasse and Raspail. Where these two thoroughfares intersect is the centre of Left Bank life, the pendant to lower Montmartre. There, instead of the quiet decency of Lavenue's or of the Closerie des Lilas, you have flaming gin or jazz palaces such as the Dôme, Rotonde and Select, which strangers imagine provide Paris with her artistic home.

142

ST. GERMAIN DES PRÉS
"In the old quarter"

Some men and a few women who really are working, who may later on make a name for themselves as artists or writers, may be found among the frequenters. But here, as at Montmartre, America provides the dominant note. Studying art in Paris would seem to be a highly popular pursuit among young Americans to-day, but even more prefer to play at it and talk about it. Long hair, dirt and eccentricity of dress are no longer deemed essential to Latin Quarter fame. There are survivals of the old 'rapins,' youths whose artistic souls find more expression in baggy trousers, outrageous hats and exotic hair-cuts than they ever manage to confide to a canvas, and you may safely lay odds that the more extravagant among them are the latest arrivals from Main Street. Most of them spend a year or two discovering that they are not Whistlers or Sargents, and then obey a paternal summons to return home and get down to 'real work.' Others remain, finding in the elusiveness of their inspiration a plausible excuse for a life of laziness in which talk and drink play a prominent part.

They haunt the Rotonde, Dôme and Select, and pursue their art to the bottom of any glass they can lay their hands on. Much more familiar to them are the 'art galleries' in bars where regular customers hang in caricature upon the wall, than the inside of any real *atelier*. They offer a picture of that most painful of all processes of decay – Youth prematurely rotting into middle age. Every now and again, a few of the '*anciens*' – men who have 'arrived' – float back to the Quarter for a night, and scandalize school-marms by the brutal *bonhomie* of their behaviour towards the Kiki, Thérèse or Olga of the moment. Every now and again, some wide-eyed youth will drift into a café on a current of misinformed illusion, and enthusiastically work his ukelele or guitar, but only so long as some *sergent de ville* disguised as a non-commissioned *maître d'hôtel* decides that the amount of drink being consumed at the tables justifies the noise. Otherwise, with what politeness may be available among the management, young Merton of the Movies will be told to take himself and his noisy jazzing, negro-spiritual-singing friends elsewhere. But on the whole, at Montparnasse as at Montmartre, the old spirit of the Quarter is dead. At any rate, in so far as Parisians are concerned, it has been swamped by money-spending foreigners un-accustomed to its ways and unversed in enjoyment's art.

With all its present-day sordidness, it is a considerable improve-ment upon the dreary make-believe of New York's Greenwich village, with its mock Old English inns, its Russian Traktirs and fake French cafés. The British student of art is present in Mont-parnasse, but in rapidly diminishing numbers, and with mood and purse chastened by war. Paris no longer holds her former place of proud supremacy in the hearts of British artists, who have seen men whose training owes nothing to Paris and all to London or Dublin — men such as Augustus John or Orpen — producing work equal to anything Paris can show. Moreover, the freedom of Quarter life does not go to British students' heads with quite the apoplectic effect it has upon many Americans. Greater familiarity enables them to manage both their oats and their legs.

The rest of the Montparnasse café crowd forms an amazing ethno-logical mixture, ranging from exotics such as the Japanese Foujita with gipsy ear-rings, to darker-tinted Mexican Indians, and includ-ing a large contingent of fresh-complexioned, blue-eyed, solid Scandinavians, who work perhaps as seriously as any other foreign community. These artistic sets are dotted here and there with writers and journalists, also mainly foreigners, and again mostly Americans, some of whom have really arrived, some of whom really are writing, but most of whom are really only talking and hoping that their masterpieces may get themselves written by miraculous means. A few among the writing set still are French. They congre-gate at the Closerie des Lilas opposite the Bal Bullier, once the hub of the Quarter's wheel of life. There used to be the head-quarters of the Prince of Poets and many another budding rhymester. Alas, the lilacs too have blossomed into an American Bar, where grey melan-choly Frenchmen sit about on high stools playing dolorously at this new life of the Quarter, and mourning the days that are gone.

Underneath this tawdry façade of jazz and make-believe are 'fine things to be done and fine things to be seen.' The sacred flame of art and thought still glows through the cinders of commercialism, but only faintly, for the verdict of Paris is become a purchaseable com-

144

modity. Art criticism is bought and sold, like bread, by the foot. Art dealers have with devastating effect applied to the sale and purchase of pictures bucket-shop methods that should make Jacob Factor modest. They acquire options, rig the market, deal in futures, and recommend certain 'lines' as being either 'sound investment' or 'good speculation,' backing up their advice with all the patter of a share-pusher.

An artist who wants to hold an exhibition in Paris has to do more than take a gallery, arrange his pictures, advertise, and invite the critics, for critics will only come in response to a gilt-edged invitation. The critic of an important Paris newspaper expects payment from the artist of at least sixty francs a line, before his critical faculties become really acute. Some will accept payment in kind in the shape of a picture, and there is indeed one well-known authority on art who every few years sells off by public auction the 'collection' he thus forms by blackmail. Partly as the result of this system, partly on account of poverty, there has of recent years been a movement among Montparnassiens to hold their own exhibitions. The natural stupidity and bad taste of the hanging committees of the *Salons* may also have had a good deal to do with the movement that has driven artists down into the market-place. While the aristocrats among them arrange for their works to hang on the walls of a friendly café, the democrats crowd into the 'foires aux croûtes' or daub fairs, and instal themselves and their works upon the pavement in a monstrous jumble sale of picturesque but pathetic failure. It is only after a visit to the daub fair that you see that even the Jury of the Independents really does draw the line somewhere. Nowhere are colours and contrasts more crude, nowhere is still-life more uproariously active and drawing more enterprising. On a bright Sunday afternoon the daub fair is thronged. Monsieur, Madame and Bébé include it in their Sunday stroll, and whereas a similar show in a London or New York thoroughfare would be greeted by loud guffaws, if it did not lead to a riot, the humble French working-man, and even the small bourgeos, has too much respect for a thing he does not pretend to understand, too much awe of the unknown, to attempt to pass judgment upon it.

In spite of all the inartistic horrors with which Paris has been afflicted in statuary and architecture – Gambetta's baggily republican marble trousers in the Tuileries, the Lavatory Renaissance of the Boulevard Raspail, the Parisian, and not by any means only the cultured inhabitant, has a feeling for art. He is certainly an assiduous visitor to his incomparable museums and art galleries, and, what is more important, sees and takes interest in what art daily life produces. At the bottom of our street is the warehouse of a manufacturer of false pearls, which usually has a knot of people outside it, not, be it said, admiring or envying the imitation pearls, but discussing the beauty of the ironwork by Brandt which has been put up to bar the windows and give an atmosphere of real worth to the Brummagem stuff inside.

In craftsmanship the Parisian man or woman excels. The men are among the finest mechanics in the world, and the artistic skill of the women has made the Paris label essential throughout the world of fashion. The men have an innate sense of touch and fitness, in dealing with such things as motor-cars and aeroplanes, which the women of Paris reveal in the curl of a hat's brim or the fall of a skirt. Parisian women are not better dressed than those of other cities. Indeed, taking all classes into account, the woman of New York wears better and more tasteful clothes than does the Parisienne. She certainly looks more closely after every detail of her toilette than does her opposite number in Paris. But all the inspiration of her clothes has its source near the banks of the Seine, where individuality is not a vice but a virtue, and where mass production, however popular it may be with regard to motor-cars, is not held in esteem when it affects frocks. It is chiefly to a power of adaptation and of individual expression that the *Parisienne* owes her reputation as the best-dressed woman in the world. The humblest workgirl, given a little time for contemplation, would turn a hard felt bowler hat into a ravishing 'confection' which would allow just the right amount of features to be seen and provide the proper frame for her uptilted chin and her rounded cheeks. To parody a popular proverb, 'It's not so much the clothes they wear, it's the cunning way they wears 'em,' which gives them their reputation. Clothe a New Yorker and a Parisienne in precisely the same gown, and one will look like a somewhat academic

THE DAUB FAIR
"A monstrous jumble sale"

goddess – a sort of bored Diana – while her French sister in the mere putting on of her dress will give it a note of challenge and that faint touch of devil that has brought so many men to 'reuin.'

Yet curiously enough the same Parisian girl who manages with sure taste and deft fingers to make the most of herself artistically, who appreciates the artistic achievements of others in the same field, tolerates an amount of domestic ugliness the equal of which could perhaps only be found in the murkiest Midland homes of England or the Middle West.

Despite the prevalence of this purely personal and decorative art, there is no artistic conscience in Paris. With but very few exceptions the architecture of the modern streets, such as the Boulevard Raspail and the extension of the Boulevard Haussmann, seems to have come out of a box of children's bricks. It is utterly banal. Most of the statues inaugurated in recent years in Paris positively disfigure the city instead of embellishing it. Here and there a shop-front or a restaurant blossoms out into something which, if not perhaps entirely successful from an artistic point of view, at any rate has the merit of effort about it. The rest of it all is hopelessly uniform and dull. There are, in the business quarters of Paris, no buildings which attempt to convey a sense of the dignity of modern commerce, of the solidity of the great banking institutions, or of the social importance of the large insurance companies of the country. The greater part of them is hidden away in buildings which could equally well serve for living-apartments, warehouses, or offices for small traders. Yet the men responsible for these new constructions are nearly all of them the product of the academic schools of Paris which, in painting, sculpture and architecture, exerted at one time an undisputed supremacy over men's minds throughout the world.

Paris may still be necessary as an experience to an artist, but it certainly is no longer essential to him from the point of view of technical training. It is good for any art student to get to know Paris life, but if he comes to Paris seeking for experience from great teachers in the Academies, whose names a few years ago were famous throughout the world, he will be disappointed. The decay of the French drawing school is doubtless largely due to the process of 'middle classification.'

This has been going on with increasing strength ever since the Revolution, and has perhaps now reached its height, since it is beginning to give birth to proletarian reaction. It is also in part to be ascribed to the economic results of war which have forced tailors as well as art professors to keep a closer eye upon their *sous*. Perhaps the students themselves are mainly responsible for the falling-off in the training which they get. Most of the well-known academies are now crowded with foreigners, mainly American, to whom the pursuit of art is a means of having a good time in Europe rather than the whole work of their lives.

Artistically, the French, and it is nowhere more noticeable than in Paris, seem to be living upon their dead selves rather than stepping upon them to higher things, and there is practically no living French artist, now that Monet is dead, who really has a world-wide reputation. There are still, however, numbers of excellent and conscientious draughtsmen, one or two good portrait-painters, and a host of witty caricaturists whose work provides the daily and the weekly papers with deft and thoroughly amusing pictorial comments on the passing phases of everyday life. They have escaped the process of commercialization which has disheartened so many men eager to work in the higher spheres of art, because, by the very ephemeral necessities of daily publication, their work cannot be stored up by a crafty picture-dealer anxious to rig the market. It has to be submitted day after day to the popular verdict. Until Paris can free herself from the stranglehold of the dealer, her influence in the world of art, now only based upon sentimental tradition, will never be recaptured.

FOLK WHO ARE MENTIONED IN THE SOCIETY COLUMNS OF THE *New York Herald* or the *Figaro* proudly consider themselves to be Parisians, even though their names proclaim them to be as much Central East as their accents betray the fact that they come from the Middle West. Paris is full of transatlantic climbers who sometimes achieve here, through local ignorance about the foreigner, the social success which they are unable to attain at home. There is nothing more amusing to any student of the great Life Book of Snobs than to see the efforts made by their compatriots to avoid the company of social detrimentals, whether gold-diggers or pork-packers, when they meet them abroad.

British society in Paris has no real existence. Our aristocracy, whether it be founded on the piratical skill of a Norman ancestor or the excellent brewing of more immediate forbears, has always vaguely felt that it alone is the 18-carat nobility. To most British aristocrats a foreign Count is no Count, and it is almost with surprise that they sometimes discover, in the *Almanach de Gotha*, families of a descent not only more distant, but even more reputable than their own. The easy alacrity with which French adventurers have snatched titles of nobility themselves does to a great extent justify the aloof attitude usually adopted by British visitors towards Parisian aristocracy. Moreover, the reign of the English *milor* is ended for ever. Russian Grand Dukes long ago took the social eminences occupied by the Lord Henry Seymours of half a century ago, and they in their turn have been ousted by Rastaquouères, Levantines, Oriental potentates and war profiteers. Practically the only Society that would gain recognition from the Lord Chamberlain in Paris, that of the *Vieille Noblesse*, is too retiring, and as a rule too poverty-stricken, to make itself visible in the glitter of Rolls-Royces and Millions which nowadays constitute fashionable life. They live in decaying town mansions, taking their dowerless spinster daughters to church at Ste.-Clotilde and vanish into further recesses of gloom in Brittany for months at a time, in summer. They refuse steadfastly to recognize that such a thing as a Republic or a Republican can exist. They are rather like retired ghosts who find their pensions inadequate. Some have disgraced themselves by manufacturing motor-cars, while others have frankly taken up the commercial development of their vineyards; – they are few.

Official Republican society is even duller. We have all heard of being as 'jolly as Kings,' but nobody has yet been found to make a song about the joviality of the President of a Republic. He, poor man, is a fairly close prisoner of his office, and has to model all his public life and most of his private existence in accordance with the dictates of the protocol, the workings of which, like those of the British Constitution, have never been properly understood by anybody. The President is housed in a palace which in exterior very faithfully reproduces the dullness of life inside. If Alice were ever to take Christopher Robin to see the changing of the *Garde Municipale* outside the Élysée they would both have a very early tea. While the Republic provides the President with a silver-breasted escort on big State occasions, and makes him wear full evening-dress at all sorts of uncomfortable daylight hours, it cannot be said to encourage him to indulge in any social magnificence. The palace is a mean-looking building of two stories composed of one small room after another. Its only redeeming feature is the garden, which runs down to the Champs Elysées, and there perhaps the only really pleasant Presidential entertainment is given – an annual children's party. Each year there are one or two official balls attended by hundreds of more people than can possibly get inside the palace with comfort, and the evening usually resolves itself into a perspiring search for refreshments and to large numbers of the guests flowing out to the café terraces in the Rue Royale to find the *coupe de Champagne* or the Bock which they have failed to discover at the Élysée. When the President entertains a foreign monarch there is a vast amount of polishing and brushing of liveries beforehand, and things are done in considerable style, but there has probably not been an instance when, after a Presidential visit to the Court of St. James, some thoroughly good Republican member of the President's suite has not somewhat ruefully remarked that there was something in Monarchy after all.

The Presidents of the Senate and the Chamber of Deputies are also committed to a certain amount of official entertaining in their rather shabby, dingy Luxembourg and Bourbon palaces. Naturally

150

most of their guests are politicians belonging to all parties and the social mixture which results is worth while studying. The Minister of Foreign Affairs is the best equipped official host. His *salons* are large, and, although his walls are hung with crimson brocaded silk, it is mercifully to a large measure concealed behind some of the finest Gobelins from the National collection. While the President of the Republic, when he gives a dinner to a visiting sovereign, has to get a cook in from one of the restaurants, at the Quai d'Orsay they have not only a minister but a chef as well.

But the real Parisians, after all is said and done, and the ones who appear to enjoy life most, are the working classes. In spite of all the prevalent 'isms,' the Parisian is not ashamed of his toil. He is sufficiently 'class-conscious,' in the sound sense of the word, not to be for ever seeking to take snobbish refuge in the black coat of the bourgeois. While it may not always be the ambition of a Paris plasterer to see his son also spend his life upon a ladder, he certainly sees no advantage in making of him an office clerk on starvation wages. To most of them a white smock or corduroys are the uniform of freedom rather than the livery of subservience. This spirit gives to the Paris streets 'a diversity of creatures' unknown to London or New York. It seems to keep alive a little bit of the old guild spirit. Jolly companions in blue jeans or in voluminous velvet breeches line the streets at midday, feeding with frank enjoyment outside small *bistros* without a thought that anyone could possibly think the worse of them because of their working garb. Even plumbers, taxi-cab-drivers and other professional *apaches* seek no sartorial anonymity. Servant-girl and cook, while generally rejecting cap and white apron, nevertheless go about their marketing without troubling to put on silk stockings and high-heeled shoes, and slop around the street hatless and in felt slippers with a string bag bulging with bread and vegetables proclaiming their occupation to every passer-by. The Parisian navvy, who politically is a desperate fellow, and is always threatening to strike, would almost rather work than cease wearing the red sash round his middle which combines the two functions of holding up his corduroys and stating his political faith.

Another corporation of Parisian workmen, that of the taxi-drivers, proclaims its Bolshevism by a more direct action. They have a lordly disregard both for their customers and for the pedestrian. When their appetite strikes noon nothing will keep them away from their food. It is indeed a wise thing for the casual visitor to Paris in search of a good and cheap meal to mark down any little restaurant which between half-past eleven and half-past twelve has a long line of idle taxicabs outside it. Russians and Central Europeans seem to have taken to taxi-driving with zest. It must be a profession which appeals to their sense of adventure, for as a rule they have carefully refrained from any study of the car they are driving, the rules of the road, geography of Paris, or of the French language. As nearly twenty per cent. of the population of Paris is foreign, they naturally stand out in considerable relief against the home background.

The colour problem has not afflicted Paris as it has the States, and Grenelle can in no way be compared with Harlem, the negro quarter of New York. But the Grenelle district has some curious fascination for the North African negro – the Kabyle – who is known generically as Sidi, because each time an Algerian or a Moor is taken to a police-station the police cannot possibly make out what his real name is and he is charged and registered as Sidi. These blackbirds are the dregs of Paris' foreign population; like Teddy Paine 'they do all the dirty work,' collecting the garbage of the capital and shovelling coal into factory furnaces in the Red belt. The coloured aristocracy, white-shirted and swallow-tailed, would certainly not even admit any racial connection with them. The black nobility is constituted by the dancers of the Folies Bergère and other music-halls and by the countless jazz bands of Montmartre. There is still quite a number of slightly less coloured, mild-mannered Annamites left over from the labour battalions who kept the road from Bar le Duc to Verdun repaired during the critical months of the war. They also, together with a few Senegalese, have settled down in Grenelle.

Many causes have contributed to swell the foreign population of Paris, the chief one being the Russian Revolution. Russian refugees have now to a great extent acclimatized themselves, and as they carry on no political conspiracies and have individually solved their

" A diversity of creatures"

economic problems they do not figure largely in the preoccupations of the police. Quite another element, and a much less controllable population, has been introduced into Paris, partly as the result of American immigration restrictions and partly as the result of political dictatorships in Italy and Spain. Anarchy has always found it easy to explain that an otherwise honest burglary is really the application of a philosophical political theory, and among the Italian and Spanish population of Paris there are many posing as victims of Mussolini's and Primo de Rivera's tyranny who are nothing but gaolbirds who have been lucky enough to get out of the cage.

All this foreign population contributes very largely to the crime statistics of Paris, and hardly a night passes without some Guiseppe, Sidi, or Carlos using the knife or a revolver.

"'Ere's a stranger; let's 'eave 'arf a brick at 'im,' has not always been the battle-cry of Parisians, nor is it entirely so to-day. While the British or American visitor who keeps a smile on his face and does not deliberately treat Parisians as though they are wild animals is seldom likely to get into trouble, there is unquestionably a strong 'foreign devil' feeling in Paris. The city, like a vain woman, is very proud of her beauty, and is apt to grow pettishly arrogant with her admirers. She is a mistress who exacts full payment in cash as well as in adulation, and should the latter ever fail she is always willing to admire herself. The journalists of Paris, frequently, are quite foolish in this matter. To question the position of Paris as the fountain-head of civilization, as the home of politeness, as the mother of all art and the only place where all men are witty and cultured and all women are beautiful and beautifully dressed, is to write yourself down a woad-stained savage from the outer marshes where people habitually use fish and dessert knives and call a serviette a napkin.

Alas and alack! every Parisienne is not a beauty and as 'swell dressers' the office-girls of New York and Washington have their Parisian sisters beaten to a 'frazzle.' An intelligent Frenchman once remarked, 'French women wear their clothes with intelligence. American women wear French clothes with distinction and English women with luck – not all of it good.' You will certainly see more pretty girls on Fifth Avenue or in Hyde Park than you will in Paris.

But in whispering that fact in these pages we are risking expulsion as 'foreign devils' who don't appreciate Paris.

The inhabitants of the capital of the Ile de France are no less insular, are indeed perhaps more insular, than are the dwellers in the British Isles, and they suffer a similar fate, for they deprive themselves of an infinite amount of pleasure and profit. Even among French artists there are few who have any notion that art exists apart from Montmartre, Montparnasse and the *ateliers*. M. Dupont rubs his eyes in surprise every now and again when the price given for a Raeburn or a Gainsborough becomes a news item. 'Hold, hold,' he says in surprise, 'those sacred animals apparently once were able to paint!' But names such as John or Orpen have never fallen on his ear, and he has not the slightest notion that Britain has developed a quite flourishing modern portrait school. Whistler is known mainly because of the extraordinary fact that his portrait of his mother has got into the Louvre.

In literature things are not much better, but there more excuse can be found for insularity in the dread difficulties of translation. The tongue of Shakespeare is not that of the Latin, and the charming books of André Maurois have probably done more to explain British character to French minds than all the works of Kipling and Jack London, who, almost alone among modern English authors, command an audience here.

Much of the 'foreign devil' feeling that has always been displayed by the Parisian is as unjust as it is illogical. In one and the same paper it has been possible to read a violent attack upon the lavish expenditure of British and American tourists in luxury restaurants, and an equally morose upbraiding of humbler Britons crowding up cheaper establishments. But, however unjust and illogical Parisian xenophobia may be, it has its natural side. Parisians not unreasonably feel hurt when they find their favourite cafés resounding with the shrill accents of New England or the long drawl of Lancashire. They resent the somewhat blatant way in which Anglo-Saxon banks exploit the best situations of their town around the Place de l'Opéra, on the boulevards and the Place Vendôme. They don't so much mind their country being more or less in pawn to foreigners, for they know they can by their own efforts redeem the pledge, but they hate being reminded of their present penury by other people's ostentatious opulence. They also object to the unconscious rudeness of the one-tongued tourist, although they themselves would be just as badly off at New York or London from a language point of view.

They feel that by some mysterious operation of the laws of economic exchange British and American visitors get something for nothing out of the country. Thus each year wild protests go up against the agents who buy turkeys in Normandy for England's Christmas dinner, or butter in Brittany, poultry from Bresse, and by the working of the law of demand and supply keep internal prices on a high level – a level which it is perfectly true the ordinary chicken-loving French household cannot reach.

Paris has long ago abandoned her right to be called the polite city of the world. Parisians jostle and push each other and their visitors off the pavement, fight for seats in 'bus or Metro with very much the same vigorous disregard for other people's feelings as is shown in similar circumstances by the inhabitants of any crowded city in the world. Democracy is not yet become a school of deportment. In the old days you were wise to be politely obsequious to your superiors, whether you were Jacques Bonhomme in the street or an ambitious young sprig at Court, for your superiors had definite ways of making themselves felt. Nowadays the 'arrivistes' of the Third Republic have shown that politeness only pays when it is a calculated act and has ceased to be a natural courtesy. A young man of brains, energy, and tact can storm nearly any Parisian citadel if he is only sufficiently ruthless and cheeky. But, curiously enough, while manners of the upper and middle bourgeois classes show distinct signs of deterioration, and while the Paris working-man and woman can be as violently vituperative as those of any capital, they have not lost the courtesy of kindness and of compassion, and the broad community of war, despite political agitations, has prevented frank personal relations between master and man, mistress and maid, from being destroyed, at any rate in small businesses and households. There both sides know that the personal comfort and prosperity of each other are interdependent, and in the average Paris flat the maid-of-all-work

155

frequently enters with disarming frankness and real kindliness into the trials or pleasures of the family she serves.

But with the foreigner matters are on a different footing. A foreigner to the Parisian will always be an inferior and unfortunate being, in that he does not happen to be French. And as a general rule they will only trouble about him, seek to understand his jargon and his ways, if there is going to be profit in the process. In this perhaps the Parisian is no better and no worse than anyone else, but as Paris exerts her charm over more people's minds than any other city in the world, she really only profiteers at the foreigner's expense upon a wider scale, for the tourist is her great market. Perhaps the Parisian attitude towards foreigners is due to slow wonder as to whether Paris is still the undisputed Queen of the World.

No TRUE SWEDE IS HAPPY OUT OF SIGHT OF WATER; NO FRENCH-man thinks life complete if he cannot see trees. Indeed, he is quite content if he can see nothing else. There are few places in the world more renowned for being on a hill than Saint-Germain-en-Laye, with its famous terrace overlooking Paris; but hardly a score of dwellings there have a farther view than the house opposite, or their own heavily-shaded lawn. Damp and mosquitoes count for nothing with the forest-loving French; and there are innumerable dark and sodden lawns, which in England would be laughing with a thousand colours, that in France are ringed with the sober richness of a triple coronal – shrubs; low trees; and high ones. It is no wonder that the French are the world's best foresters; they feel actual personal affection for trees.

It is natural that a nation devoted to 'dreamy, gloomy, friendly' trees should have a capital decorated with them; and Paris has sylvan glades in her very midst. The plantations of the boulevards are without grandeur, though they have charm; but the green tunnel of the Avenue Henri-Martin on a summer's day, its golden sadness in autumn, its shout of youth in spring, and its tracery of shadow, as delicate as sea-weed, in winter, are worthy of the stateliest country palace in the world. On a hot day it so 'annihilates all that's made to a green thought in a green shade' that if one did stumble on a melon as one passed it would hardly be surprising, even though one were merely hastening to the tram-stop.

The trees here are so thick that the houses are almost invisible. In the Avenue des Champs Elysées one cannot forget houses; but in the Champs Elysées themselves, down towards the Place de la Concorde, trees and children rule all.

Here is the magnolia which celebrates the turn of the year from cold to warm by such a largesse as emperors know not. One day it is a brown-branched tree with long buds of a coldish pink, tight-closed, set upon it like unlit candles. Only a few hours later it has opened wide a thousand creamy cups of fragrance to a love-scene with the sun; tree and sun each trying to catch and keep all of the other that it can, both knowing that so much loveliness must be travelling to the shadows.

157

Here is the Guignol, where French children learn to laugh at the policeman, though they know they must never do it anywhere else. Here is a roundabout of little horses, even now turned by a hard-working man who grinds a handle and a tune. Here are the cheerful young trees doing their best to look as big as their elders, and planted on the site of the 'Jardin de Paris,' the Ranelagh of love-making and fairy-lamps which disappeared only a few years ago.

Here are the few solemn big trees which survived the camp of the wild Cossacks of 1814. Their horses ate the bark, their fires burned the foliage, the grass, and the shrubs; and Louis XVIII, repairing the damage, thus accidentally became the first architect of a street as proud as any in Europe. Le Nôtre's straight avenue gave him his groundwork, and the marshes and ponds and thickets between which it ran, where trees grew as they do in the country, gave place to ordered paths and shaded drives. Torchlight banquets must vanish from this henceforth urban roadway. If Napoleon returned and wanted to feast his twelve thousand veterans after Iéna he would have to find another place for them. But what a stretch of dead tree that was under the living branches, when the wooden tables extended for more than a mile from the Concorde to the rising Arc de Triomphe and back, and the *grognards* beat upon them with their wood-handled knives at the name of Napoleon!

The Avenue du Bois had not been thought of then. To-day it is full of wonderful exotic trees, so rare that their names (in careful Latin) are pinned to the trunks or displayed in little iron frames at their feet. Under them, walk children almost as exotic as they; but the trees have natural foliage and strange names, and the opposite is true of the children. They are called Jeanne or Augustine or Achille or Georges, but put forth unnatural leaves of frilled silk and embroidered satin and gold-bedecked velvet. French children are dressed more simply now than before the war, especially on week-days, but their best clothes are still elaborate enough to be worn by their mothers. In the Avenue du Bois, some are wheeled in lacquer carriages under ermine coverlets. Others walk sedately, and if a very small one squatters down upon his or her little silk-clad haunches, to come to close quarters with a specially friendly-coloured pebble, the appalled voice of a 'neursse anglaise' (this is not a mother-street) soon recalls the horrid fact that in the classes which have taken silk the utmost dignity, even at the age of three, is necessary. Some of the trees, gazing down at their labels and their restricted lawns, look a little as if they also had been put into crêpe de Chine knickers and found them pretentious nuisances.

Still, the Avenue du Bois is as fine as the vanguard of an army, if as self-conscious. With a flourish and a rustle of its own foreign standards it leads into the very midst of Paris the great and endless army of the French woodlands. It stands peering through the Arch down to the Tuileries, and along to the Bois de Vincennes, whispering, 'Come along, come along! This upstart city has kept us apart long enough. Let's roll over it! I'm ready when you are. We are the forests of France!'

A herald of this message, a flourishing young tree at least three feet high, grew until lately in a corner of the roof of the Louvre. Some vagary of wind had arrested the seed-messenger; or perhaps it was sheer defiance that rooted it there, that it might show how old crumbling stone may with luck become as useful as good earth. That is a witty lesson to read to humans, who can hardly ever see or put five trees together, without feeling an itch to erect a stone statue within their arc.

There is something really approaching tree-worship in Paris. In the Boulevard Raspail there is a house as misshapen as Quasimodo, because it is built round a tree planted by Victor Hugo; and when a landlord bows to anything which is going to take from him many feet of land as dear as rubies, it is certain that he is bowing to a god. This is not the only instance; in the Avenue du Parc-Montsouris there is a house similarly deformed in favour of a tree, and there may be others. A little more, and Paris would build round Ygdrasil. Perhaps she is only prevented from having a hearth-tree as real as Sieglinde's by a recognition of the fact that open-air and rain and all that range of natural medicaments are necessary for trees.

Yet with all her love of them Paris has nothing to show like the great elms and planes and sycamores of London squares; nor any green stretch comparable with the unbroken open spaces from Notting Hill to Westminster. The Bois de Boulogne is infinitely more rural than a London park; but it is on the very outskirts of the city. The Champ Elysées, the Tuileries, the Luxembourg, the Palais Royal and the Parc Monceau all put together, would fit into Regent's Park and leave handsome trimmings *and* the Zoo. There are small trees neatly marshalled round the edge of the Place des Vosges, and the trees along the boulevards are welcome indeed in a wilderness of stone and stucco; but there are no Paris trees like the gentle giants of Lincoln's Inn Fields or Berkeley Square.

There are birds in Paris, but not so many as in London. There are plenty of sparrows in the public gardens, and in the unexpected green places of the city there is here a blackbird or there a thrush. But in France as a whole, full as she is of forests, bird-life is rarer than in England. Paris has a good many pigeons, but none of the parks in her central quarters can offer a quarter of the nature-study of Regent's Park or Kensington Gardens.

Paris loves trees and children — one cannot think for two minutes of either subject without finding the other equally present to the mind — and she sacrifices herself to both. But she brings up her trees better than her children, for she does not spoil them. She lops them, and prunes them, and stakes them against the wind, and generally sergeant-majors them for their own good. Her children she indulges — they are rarer than her trees, and not so easily or so plentifully produced, let alone so cheaply brought to a fruitful maturity.

Americans in Paris have occasionally protested with unrestrained vigour against the spectacle of white girls dancing with negroes. They have even gone so far as to wrest the ivory girls from the ebony arms of their chosen partners. Evidently these quixotes have been suffering the pangs which visit the breast of the Anglo-Saxon visitor to France, in the presence of the French boy and his mother. To see a lad, somewhere between eight and eighteen, who is occasionally if not often as rosy as a pippin, as plump of leg and cheek as a partridge, sitting down in an omnibus or tram or train, while his tired mother swings on her feet from whatever support she can find — straps being an unknown luxury here — is trying to the temper.

It is not the child's fault; his mother has asked him to be a demi-

THE LUXEMBOURG
"Paris loves trees and children"

god, and few of us, at any age, can refuse such an invitation. At the age of minus nine months, when this invitation was first issued, it amounted to a royal command. On the other hand, one can hardly blame the French mother for being perfectly satisfied with her off-spring. About the year 1900 she was standing patiently in a crowded Underground train, while a nine-or-ten-year-old sat fatly by her side, who was afterwards to be one of the soldiers of Verdun – one of those old soldiers in their early twenties who came to Paris on leave at the end of the torment of 1916; their eyes sunk in their heads, and their glances, as they strolled along the boulevards, or mechanically army-stepped down the Rue Royale, slipping vaguely away from the prettiest girl, the friendliest smile, the heartiest invitation. Perhaps military training, let alone the fire-baptism of Verdun, puts right a French mother's indulgence. Nothing can prevent the Briton in Paris from resenting the attitude of the growing French boy (girls are more rationally treated) to his mother and sisters; but nothing should prevent the reflection that the intolerably impertin-ent stripling of 1927 is possibly the son of a hero of 1916 who was himself an intolerably impertinent stripling in 1900.

Perhaps it is not fair to take children at the age of ten years. They are just entering on that difficult and tumultuous decade which is the middle-age of youth, and is every whit as new, as discon-certing, as humiliating, and as interesting as the middle-age of life.

The boys are also subject to foreign criticism because of their clothes. This is the fault of the foreign critics, who have no right to object if telescopic youths wear bare knees while growing. Quite elderly boys wear bare knees and socks, even when they overtop their fathers by inches; but they are not necessarily to be called 'Cissie,' as a trousered foreign schoolmate may perhaps discover on trial; on the other hand, they may really be soft and mother's darlings, and yet be the hardest of hard stuff in a year or two.

The French boy of intermediate age cannot profitably be dis-cussed. His manners and his clothes obscure him from the view of his foreign contemporaries. He cannot see them either. He knows more than they do, and studies harder, and nobody tells him that his socks look silly to them, and that no chap lets his mother stand while he sits. They are query-marks to each other.

Younger French children are easier to understand. And so very easy to love! Such solemn scraps of adored humanity! French babies are hardly ever less than fifty years old. They all have charge of their parents, and give royal assent to the games these parents play, such as feeding and dressing one, and requiring to be taken to the nearest public garden after lunch, where they have the quaintest pastimes with needles and thread, while one works hard at sand-castles and staring at the other boy.

It's a hard-worked life and a dusty one. As a responsible child of a family one cannot walk on the grass, it would be such a bad example to Maman. But then, on the whole she is so very good – she carries the purse, and sometimes hires a white or even a red-sailed boat for one to send adventuring on the pond. Or, at the kiosk up among the chestnuts, she buys one a bright ball in a brighter net-bag. Ages ago, when one was really small, it would have been five splendid feathers on a stick, blowing round and round like brothers of a rainbow. Or the lovely, lovely *lovely* little yellow wheel-barrow! If only they would let one carry away sand, or even dust! Only if they did, the concierge wouldn't like it. And what she says is more than anything anyone else ever said. Maman consequently can't buy the darling wheelbarrow, but a ball or a little trumpet she is quite ready for. (Not for twenty years will one know how she feels about the trumpet.) So the least one can do now is to down spade from time to time, and go and ask her if that lovely needlework or knitting or crochet is for you or for her – knowing the answer!

Then the moment comes when she opens the basket at her side; a brown one, turned bronze by the flicker of leaves overhead. Out comes a sandwich; and very nice too – this morning's crisp bread with some cold meat from lunch between. And there's going to be some chocolate after. But oh, what is this fragrance that steals upon the nose?

Suddenly one is very small and young and dependent. If Maman is not hungry, will she sniff it as she should? Or will she, if not feeling robust, merely say 'Pah!' and move farther off? Could she possibly do such a thing unless feeling really bilious, when this smell, this odour, this perfume, this aroma, this fragrance, is embalming the air?

It comes from a square of black iron, fixed under a tree near by. Everything is under trees here. The whole world is wingle wongle with light and shade; even Maman's stitch-game has sometimes to be held to the mid-path light for surety. The black square has heat in it, and a man with a great bowl, full of stuff that looks like cream, drops it on hot irons and thrusts them in, and presently pulls them out, and sugars the thin, golden crust, and hands it over, with a foaming cool beaker of milk.

Gaufres and milk under the trees – who can forget the strange spell of that hot fragrance in the cool open air, that will to the end of one's life have reference only and wholly to these days of youth? Ever greener with age and damp were the pedestals of statues round which one played. Somewhere in the upper air stone figures of queens and goddesses soared, like mountains or Eiffel Towers or the tallest stories of one's house. But the dusty ground, the shuttle-work of voices among Maman and her neighbours, the white needlework, the boat, the pond, and the hot crisp smell of baking, the rumbling of trams and 'buses, the cropped formal trees along the alleys, the occasional thickets in neglected corners, the deeper and wider shade of some bigger trees, and the swinging tesselation when the breeze blew among the shadows – these are the inalienable heritage of the Paris child.

They are known even to the guttersnipe of Montmartre, who has for playthings instead of spade and sand, boat and pond, the mason's overnight leavings of plaster and lime and bricks. The trams cannot get up the hill, and even the 'buses come to a grumbling stop far below; but there is a constant noise of motor-coaches and taxis, and foreign footsteps and the sleek voice of the guide is heard in the land. Poulbot's children are very strange and unlikely to English eyes, for could anything so young be so old? Only the Cockney child of the Dickens period, or the Poulbot child of Montmartre.

The Poulbot child plays among the housebreaker's ruins and the mason's promise as earnestly as if he were making sand-houses upon

163

the shores of ocean, with sea-breezes blowing upon him, pure with three thousand miles of landlessness; he leads his little troop to combat, in paper helmets, as dauntlessly as Antony. Nobody knows what language Antony used in stress of battle; it is fortunate, perhaps, that the average visitor to Montmartre knows almost as little what the Poulbot child is saying, for his vocabulary is less gentle than direct. On the other hand, the French of the Parc Monceau child has an exquisite precision unknown to the nations which do not place their words well forward between lips and teeth. The French baby could not say a simple English word like 'since' without practice; but visiting Chancellors and Ministers and Ambassadors and Plenipotentiaries would give half the syllables of their titles to be able to say 'depuis' as correctly.

The wealthy Paris child, to be studied in the Avenue du Bois or the Parc Monceau, differs but little from wealthy children in other capitals, save that the girls are so elaborately clothed. A good saleswoman in a Paris shop would not dream of presenting to a British mother the clothing intended for wear by a young French lady of four or six; which, to that customer's ideas, needs only to be larger in order to suit a lady of from forty to sixty.

The real Paris child is neither the lace-ridden promenader under the exotic trees of the Avenue, nor the precocious sparrow of Poulbot's Montmartre; but the child of the classes which range from the families of doctors and lawyers to the rag-picker's babies who must learn to be alone in the dark, because their parents must need leave them in the small hours; the classes which have their centre somewhere about the tradesman class in a well-to-do delivery district. The typical Paris boy is the son of the concierge in a decent residential house. He is about eight as a rule, as clean as an apple, with a rigorously cropped head, and arrayed in thick, sturdy clothes, covered by a black or checked red and white overall, with a leather belt through which his little hands are thrust when he stands in his doorway to survey the great world. He has a little stool, on which he sits for hours on a fine day, just by the door, fabricating long, long games that involve occasional excursions along the pavement, which are perhaps journeys to China, or ticket-collecting expeditions down the length of a train, or visits made by himself (now President of the Republic), to foreign capitals amid the respectful plaudits of untold multitudes; or, when Pegasus is lazy, merely the postman's round, delivering letters of great import.

This child lives, as a rule, in a room very little larger than the huge bed it contains, often without any direct light or air, and usually enlivened by a constant smell of food. He is accustomed to visitors, for every sort of face is thrust in at the door, and every sort of voice asks his mother for the different people in the house. This is amusing; when other children are having their food or doing their lessons in the dullest seclusion, the little son of the concierge lifts his round eyes over book or plate, and examines with perfect security, in his own home, the interesting strangers who can only be inspected by less fortunate comrades in the open air, where mothers are not.

One summer dusk, when the air was the colour of a pansy, a boy of seven had put forth into the spaces of a quiet square near the home-door. He was on hands and knees in the middle of the street, intent on some stage of a game as engrossing to him as life was to d'Artagnan, when a passer-by who considered a roadway, even a quiet one, a bad place for absorbed little boys, went up to him and touched him on the shoulder. He looked up. He saw no benevolent stranger, merely desirous that he should not be run over. He saw a huge man, yards high, who had appeared without sound behind him, as though materialized from the rich-coloured twilight; a man with an ivory face, very pointed, and a little devilish pointed black beard and pointed black moustaches; with great bellying red knickers and a blue gold-embroidered coat, and a huge white cloak; with very white teeth, and very piercing eyes, and very long arms; a man who loomed over him like a mountain, or a genie. If ever a boy was justified in emitting a yell for his mother and departing like an arrow from the purple air to the lit indoors, that boy was. The Zouave went his way with a rueful grin, and Lucien was left to the lighted safeties of the home-table, whence could be viewed with perfect calm even the most unexpected and gigantic figures.

There is one class of child in Paris who cannot be looked upon with cheerfulness. He is from eleven to fifteen years old, and he works in the smaller sort of restaurant, either as a *chasseur* or a *piccolo*. As a *chasseur*, he wears a uniform made for a boy of a different shape and size than his own, and ready-made boots with soles thicker than nursery bread-and-butter, and voices louder than the creaking door on which he leans between running messages. As a *piccolo*, his duty is to wear bulgy evening dress, and to do odd jobs for all the waiters, and to answer to the gentle name of 'little one,' in Italian, emitted in every tone between desperation and fury. He must carry mountains of plates through swing-doors, between and round the legs of his masters, across restaurants hotter than the Sahara into sculleries colder than the Pole; he must know where every one and everything is; he must never break anything, nor deny that he has if a waiter says so; he must never sleep, never sit down, and never have an ache in his feet or his heart or his stomach, lest it inconvenience his many masters. And he must never, never receive a tip, nor look enviously at the other tired baby, the *chasseur*, who may. These are children very pitiful to see. Their hours are abominably long, and as the evening wears on, and their eyes are so swollen with fatigue that the poor little faces look as if they had been crying for hours, their lumpy uniforms and over-large evening dress can be mentally obliterated, and there remain only two small boys, dead-tired, rather bullied, and just longing to be where many much older children are, both richer and poorer; rolled in the velvet of sleep upon their pillows.

To the physical fatigue of his job the small *chasseur* has to add another disadvantage: he learns a great deal more than he has any need to know of the seamy side of human nature. At twelve he has the knowledge of a fast-living man of fifty: Poll Sweedlepipe's Mr. Bailey was an ignoramus beside him. The fatigue on the worn little face is not all physical; he is already tired of a life he knows at second-hand and is years too young to understand. The little son of the concierge, for all his acquaintance with strange faces and voices, is a hermit in comparison with the *chasseur* of a Paris restaurant.

The son of the concierge has never heard of a nursery; but in that he resembles all but the very wealthiest children of France. A French child in a roomy country-house is usually with its parents in their living-rooms; in a Paris flat it and they have no corner to themselves, and the child is falling over the father's directory while the parent is stepping more delicately than Agag among the toys upon the floor. 'They all lived together in a little crooked house,' says the old rhyme. The Paris house is far from crooked; it is as rectangular as architects and striped wall-papers can make it; but the intensity with which Monsieur, Madame et Bébé live together is wonderful. They are never without each other. It is not surprising that the Paris child is old for its age. It lives among grown-ups; it sits up to late dinner, eating all that the parents eat and drinking beer or wine; it is a solemn-eyed party to every discussion of business or politics, dress, or housekeeping, and knows more of parties and wages, exchange and Parliament, than does the average mature Englishman. As a rule, it is that wistful creature, an only child; but even given a sister or a brother, or two of them (a family of three is officially in France a 'famille nombreuse'), the conditions remain the same.

Hence the alternate spoiling and drilling of Paris children; hence their certainty of godhead, swiftly followed by the temporary degradation of a slap or a shake; hence scenes of tears and temper; hence pale cheeks and tired eyes; hence year upon year of close-packed memories of love and home, keeping the child's heart all its life a happy captive to French kin-worship.

As one grows older one learns that no other cellar can so profitably be laid down for future enjoyment as the Remember cellar. Here's a fine bin of Star-of-Bethlehem, a slow-maturing wine from the Nuits-St.-Berceau vineyard, to be sparingly used on special occasions. Here's that very sound lot of Robin-Run-the-Hedge, Ecolier Frères, semi-sparkling, red-foil, a bit harsh on the palate, but softening with time. Here's a Traveller's Joy, Foyer et Fils, specially intended for use in strange countries; a robust wine, much in request for after-dinner consumption, with a superb bouquet, and of the richest ruby when held to the light. Here is Old Man's Beard, Château Jeunet, a wine for kings. And here, above all, in huge quantities, is a Vin Rosé, d'Antan-Bonheur et Cie, for everyday drinking, with or without water, at any meal, in any place, with any friend, or alone. Such a cellar the wise establish; but a French mother sees to it that her children find it ready for them before ever

167

they go out into the world. No vintage will ever be the same to their palates as those she chose for them in childhood as carefully as later she arranged their marriages.

This system of living in the family pocket makes French children very old for their ages. They are dead serious as they watch a frivolous world walk past, while they play under the trees in the Luxembourg or the Tuileries, or one of the little unexpected green spots of Paris, such as the Parc Royal – a tiny space in the crowded Marais – a relic of the royal splendours of the Parc des Tournelles, which was itself a relic of primeval forest, pruned into the service of kings and queens as proud and as brave and as wicked and as fascinating as if they had lived in fairy-tales, instead of drawing their swords or trailing their rich robes over this very spot.

The Republican babies of to-day care nothing for the great invisible tapestry of the past that hangs behind them as they trade pebbles and sand to each other, for all the world like the merchants who till yesterday marketed diamonds in the Rue Lafayette.

Commerce has invaded the games of the Paris child to a great extent, which is comprehensible when one remembers that his attention is daily given to the conversation of his parents. Serious, attentive creatures, these Paris children, even – or especially – when at play. But when they do laugh it is a shower of silver. Usually it is a beautiful sound in itself, but nearly always, whether harmonious or not, it wells so directly from that happy spot in the heart where we keep real laughter that within earshot the grumpiest brows unfold and the saddest lips turn upwards.

The Paris child is very easy to amuse. There are cheap cinemas in every quarter (in the centre there are two special cinemas for children, but their performances are not very frequent), and there are some sad animals in the Jardin des Plantes and the Jardin d'Acclimatation, though llama-rides and elephant-rides are among the things killed by the War.

The Paris boy and girl have never heard of pantomime, and such an institution as Drury Lane on Boxing Day is still in Paris where America was for Europe before Columbus. 'Principal boys' are more incomprehensible than mathematics to them; the Dan Lenos of France address themselves to adults, the 'transformation scene' is only attempted by music-halls, and the Harlequinade is an affair for Nice and other Carnival towns.

On the other hand, the Circus is as much appreciated in France as it was in England up to thirty years ago. In Paris there are three or four circuses almost permanently playing, and, although a touch of the music-hall has crept into their programmes, they are in the main real circuses, with performing animals, both wild and tame, equestrian feats, and, above all, clowns. The three Fratellini brothers are the crown and glory of Paris clowning; but when Foottit died a few years ago it was evident that, even in this city of short memories, the children who saw his fooling with Chocolat remembered it still in their middle age.

Fairy-plays are almost unknown. Peter Pan never yet captured the heart of any French child, who is more likely to applaud an American film of adventure than to clap its hands in token that it believes in fairies.

'Christmas Programmes' are arranged in Paris by one or two theatres, but it by no means follows that they are meant for children, or are even gay. What a Christmas Eve that was when one took a heavy-hearted widow to see Cocteau's 'Antigone,' and found that in honour of the day the programme had been switched to De Musset's endless picture of the miseries of a young lady who fell in love with a monk, and finally, but far too long afterwards, committed suicide, apparently because she hadn't the sense to take a good long walk and enter her name for the local tennis tournament!

But even if the Paris theatre catered for children, it would cost money, and the typical French infant is encouraged to prefer, or at any rate to accept cheerfully, entertainments which make no inroads on the slender purse of a country where a Field-marshal earns less than many a clerk, and the President himself, before the War, was remunerated at the rate of 40,000, now worth one-fifth of that sum, and not augmented.

France is thrifty because she has to be, in view of her small salaries; and thrift grows upon a community as heartily as a weed, till sometimes, like a weed, it threatens to choke the other plants.

169

In any case, whether parents are comfortably off or struggling, the children are taught modesty in their desires.

They have various free shows. During December the big department-stores have windows specially decked for them, and wooden barriers have to be erected, with live policemen at both ends, to keep the gazing public, which is largely adult, out of the way of the hurrying public. In the autumn there is the Concours Lépine, which used to be a worthy successor of the mediaeval Toy Fair on the Pont Neuf, and still has entrancing playthings to show, although nowadays the household contrivance threatens to swamp the toys.

Once a year the children have a great festival. On the day of their first communion the world is theirs. They are then between eight and eleven years old, and the most earnest of them cannot probably understand very much of what the mystery means; but they are given presents, and blessed, and publicly loved by all. After the tremendous ceremony of the morning, all mothers and aunts spend the afternoon proudly walking the streets till the deeply-interesting hour of the afternoon-party; fathers and uncles then accrue, and everything becomes so magnificent that only fatigue could end it. On these days the streets are decorated by little boys far too Latin to feel or look foolish because large, fringed bows of white satin adorn their left arms, and little girls so small and proud that every heart melts to them. They are dressed in white from head to foot – literally, because the Roman Catholic Church does not approve of ladies' legs, even when the ladies are only eight; so the tucked voluminous white frock must almost touch the ground. The wreath of white muslin roses binds up the hair (which must not float on this solemn day), and, since the season is spring, the splendid snowiness of this adornment must sometimes be completed by the overcoat of Papa, or the cosy shawl of Grand'maman. 'Les Premières Communions' are among the jewels of the pageantry of Paris streets, and one has but to look at the tired but unbending pride of the little faces to see that emperors might envy that day's throne.

The next day, in knickers and blouse, in short frock and long legs, the children play again under the cheerful sun-tangled trees of their Paris.

SATAN CERTAINLY KNEW HIS BUSINESS AS A PSYCHOLOGIST WHEN HE appreciated the value of high places as a jumping-off ground for sinners of greed or of ambition. It is perhaps partly because Paris can be seen that the idea of her conquest makes such an appeal both to men and women. Happier than London, she has a number of points, both in the city itself and around it, from which can be seen spread out in the valley the squalor and beauty, opulence and industry, of the capital. The terrace of that Byzantine bubble, the Sacré Cœur, commands a close though lofty view of the city's myriad spires. At night great *barrettes* of multi-coloured lights glow like jewels upon the black velvet of darkness, marking the main thoroughfares, along which pass uncertain streams of traffic lights. Railway signals wink and flicker far away, pointing to the great faintly-illumined hump of the Gare du Nord, squatting like a Thermite Queen in the middle of her lover-slaves. Further away are dark interruptions on the moonlit skyline; the basilica behind is tangled in stars, and from below the heavy murmur of life mounts up to Montmartre. Every now and again the shriek of a railway whistle is caught by a capricious gust of wind and megaphoned through the night. In gaps of silence, when even the city seems to hold its breath, the dull *bourdon* of an organ sounds from within the church.

This prospect of Paris is emotionally impressive, but it is much more restricted than the view from the heights of St.-Cloud, just outside the city limits, on the left bank of the Seine Valley, in the melancholy frame of the old clipped trees of a vanished palace and an abandoned park. There the precision of the topiarist, combined with the graceful splendour of the formal French landscape gardens, contrasts with leafy disorders, with growth and decay. The dancing limbs of marble nymphs are covered with moss. Time has all but effaced the sculptured stories on urn and frieze. The château itself is but a memory of the bombardment which destroyed it when the King of Prussia, Bismarck, and Moltke from the height gloated over the besieged city at their feet, which they were bombarding in much the same circumstances, at a range of two or three miles, as Big Bertha did from twenty times the distance nearly fifty years later. The long, high avenues of trees all lead the eye to something.

Some end in a fountain, others in a grassy setting for the antics of satyr or faun. So old, so heavily-leaved are the trees, that even on the sunniest day the shade of those tunnels cut through dark-green forest is unbroken.

The finest of them ends on a terrace hanging over Paris. Leaning over the balustrade, you have behind you melancholy memories of history, the quiet rustling of woodland life, the song of birds. From below, just across the river, comes the hot panting of steam, the grunting and groaning of mass production. In the haze of smoke and heat even that great steel spider, the Eiffel Tower, acquires merit, and the fake orientalism of the Trocadéro's twin towers is softened almost to beauty. The Arc de Triomphe, the Panthéon, the Invalides, Notre-Dame and the cupola of the Sacré Cœur, stand out from the sea of masonry, white like the crests of waves. But it is the forest of chimney-stacks that symbolizes more accurately the Paris of to-day.

St.-Cloud, despite its haunting charm and its closeness to Paris, is little favoured by the people, except for marriage festivals. It has long been almost a tradition for the bride in her vestal finery, the groom in his dreadful evening-clothes, seated in a barouche lined with white satin and laden with flowers, to drive with their guests through the Bois de Boulogne to a wedding-feast and dance at St.-Cloud, where at the foot of the heights there is a cluster of open-air restaurants which cater for 'noces' to suit all pockets. These parties usually start in the most frozen French family formality, and end, thanks to the thawing influence which even a mediocre 'Mousseux' seems to have upon a wedding-party, in old Tante Elise becoming decently Rabelaisienne in her reminiscences, in furtive hand-pressing and giggling among the young folk, and in much unmusical meandering among the mournful melodies that please Parisians when they are really living up to their reputation for gaiety.

Robinson, to the south of Paris, is a much more popular spot on a bright Sunday. It derives its name from that Swiss family of competent prigs who had a penchant for living in tree-tops. At Robinson the lover and his lass can caress in the discreet comfort of innumerable rustic châlets, they can dine in the leafy seclusion of a

"In a melancholy frame of old clipped trees"

quite a note of colour to the drabness of the Paris termini on Sundays. Shooting has a peculiar attraction for the Parisian. Whilst there are a few well-preserved estates, such as that of the Rothschilds at Ferrières, the country as a whole is very bare of game, and shooting rights can be obtained for very little over a few fields, while perhaps a small wood can be obtained for an unimportant sum. The local butcher, baker and candlestick-maker usually combine with a few friends from Paris to rent their shooting, and tremendous are the stories that result. The well-clad shooting-party, with butts, beaters, loaders and perfectly bred and trained dogs, probably gets less out of a week on the moors than the Parisians do from their Sunday in the country, with an incredible mongrel who understands but little of what is going on, save that he is out among new and vastly interesting smells and is therefore entitled to bark and run about to his heart's content. Their game-bags are never fuller than they are just before the *casse croûte*. Out of them, long before midday, comes a succulent selection of sausages, of garlic-perfumed *paté*, crisp golden bread, and a bottle or two of the 'jolly little white wine of the country.'

Game is scarce, and the lack of protection given to bird-life would make Viscount Grey greyer. The guns blaze away at everything that creeps, crawls, runs or flies. Larks unfortunately, on account of their gastronomical qualities, are not immune, and a singular device called the *Miroir* is used to attract them to the guns. It consists of a large shiny bit of tin, shaped rather like an aeroplane propeller, which by rope is made to whirl around. The flash of it in the sunshine will bring larks from the highest heavens within range of the waiting guns. Another somewhat similar contraption, called the *Grand Duc* for mysterious reasons, is formed by a large and rough dummy owl mounted on a swivel. When moved about, it is sufficiently strange and lifelike to attract the attention of hawks or other birds of prey that may be in the neighbourhood. They swoop down upon it and, within a few yards of their prey, in panic check their flight, and fluttering in their desperate attempt to backwater are an easy mark. Rabbit is the chief bag, however, and if at the end of a long day in the open M. Dupont returns to Paris with a hare, or, rarer still, a pheasant, in his bag his sportsman's pride will overcome tree-top to which their meal is hoisted in baskets by rope and pulley. Such privacy is, however, for the sophisticated few, for the Parisian of the working-class, like the coster and his donah, does not regard affection as a necessarily shameful affair to be only illicitly expressed. For the girls there are swings, while their swains can display their strength and skill on all sorts of antiquated slot-machines, in climbing ropes, or on the parallel bars. But the real thing to do at Robinson is to ride a horse or a donkey, and to persuade your girl, usually timid and always inappropriately dressed, to do likewise. Heaven knows the steeds are sedate and the donkeys docile, but even so, Jean generally finds an extreme difficulty in keeping away from the neck of his mount, whilst Louise is soon made aware by amused glances or shrieks of laughter as she is carried up the road that the length of her leg is in direct ratio to the shortness of her skirt. All this seems, no doubt, in shocking taste, but it is all done with the frankness and open enjoyment that distinguish the relaxations of simple folk the world over, and they certainly get more fun out of their Sundays than do their Parisian 'patrons' who, in their cars, are devouring dust and kilometres on their way to some Norman 'hostellerie,' whose bill is as faked as its antiquity.

The great Sunday amusement of the masses is to stroll round the boulevards with as large a family group as can be mustered, and to sit on a café terrace, taking hours over the consumption of a *bock* or a grenadine. Vincennes on the east and the Bois de Boulogne on the west are also well patronized by family parties, who play games of strange tennis and football on the grass and picnic under the trees.

It is sometimes said that sport in France is still at the bicycle stage of development; but although cycle races on the rack and on the road still retain in France a popularity which has long ago waned elsewhere, the remark is now essentially untrue. Sport of all kinds plays a very large part in a Parisian's life, as in recent years has been well advertised to the world by Carpentier in boxing, by Suzanne Lenglen, Lacoste and Borotra in tennis, by the defeat of England at Rugby football, and by the number of French-owned and French-bred winners on our British turf.

All this sporting activity is foreign in its origin, for, curiously enough, none of the local games, such as the Basque pelota, has spread beyond the restricted limits of its *petite patrie* to become a national game. Curiously enough, it is perhaps the most definitely foreign sport – that of horse-racing – that has made the biggest appeal to the people of Paris, who from a racing point of view are infinitely better catered for than Londoners. Within the limits of the city itself, in the Bois de Boulogne, is the magnificent course of Longchamps, where during the flat season there is racing on Sundays. There also is Auteuil, where jumping fixtures are held. Within easy bus distance of the Parisian are Vincennes (for trotting), Le Tremblay, St.-Cloud, Maisons Laffitte, Enghien, while Chantilly, the Newmarket of France, is but twenty-five miles away. It is there that the French Derby and the French Oaks are run; but Chantilly, from a racing point of view, is of much less interest than are Longchamps and Auteuil, where the Grand Prix and the Grand Steeplechase take place. It is there that luxury Paris is seen at its best. The green lawns, set in the beauty of the Bois de Boulogne, are decked with all that Paris can produce of smartness, loveliness and fashion. The big dressmakers are all represented by bevies of mannequins, who stroll, splendidly or pertly after their style, between the flower-beds, swaying at the hips with their professional gait. Stage beauties also find the races an excellent advertising medium for their notoriety, and the *grande cocotte* is to be seen in considerable numbers. Mere man makes no attempt to rival this feminine display, and the critic of *The Tailor & Cutter* would deplore the scarcity of the morning-coat and topper and the ill-bred prevalence of 'plus fours,' Oxford bags and other garments of the tourist. Indeed, only a few members of the Jockey Club itself remain faithful to the silk or the Ascot hat. There are not the club enclosures to be found on English courses, but their place is to a minor degree taken by the official tribunes reserved for members of Parliament, the Municipality, etc. The crowd is on the whole very much better than at English meetings, and there are no organized gangs of turf ruffians. Credit for this is given mainly to the outlawing of the bookmaker and the introduction of the Pari-Mutuel system. So peaceful and orderly are the crowds on both sides of the course that Monsieur and Madame do not hesitate to take Bébé with them, especially as small children are admitted free of charge. There are even child mannequins for infantile fashions!

While the Parisian likes a day at the races, the sport which most inflames his enthusiasm is bicycle-racing. For every French lad who dreams of becoming a successful jockey, there are thousands whose ambition it is to pedal their way to fame through the incredible endurance test of the Tour de France, which for weeks keeps the whole country in suspense, while it follows the fortunes of its favourites as they laboriously push their way through the Pyrenees and across the Alps. In Paris the great popular sporting event is the Six Days' Cycle Race at the Vélodrôme d'Hiver, where night after night at the sprint hour, after the theatres have emptied, between twenty and thirty thousand people gather round the polished bowl of the track, hypnotized by the whirling dervishes on wheels struggling to win the sprint premiums offered by the Dolly Sisters or some equally typical Parisian music-hall celebrity. The *chic monde* is noticeably absent. A few people of the *monde* look in after the theatre out of curiosity, but most of the supper-parties in the boxes in the centre of the ring belong to ill-defined circles of the theatrical world. It is the people's sport, and it is not surprising that half the Garde Republicaine and hundreds of police are on duty outside and inside until the building is cleared for cleaning, and the weary riders, still pedalling, but very lazily, read their letters and talk among themselves as they pass slowly round the deserted track. Every kind of Apache muffler, every lad of the *casquette* brigade is there, and ferocious critics they are when they suspect racers of splitting up the prizes offered for sprints among themselves.

Another favourite occupation of Parisians is fishing. Hundreds of men, and women too, spend their whole Sundays along the quayside of the Seine with ten-foot rod, horse-hair line and a maggot, hopeful that the day may dawn when some minute gudgeon or roach may get sufficiently tired of life to commit suicide. The professional garb for this patient sport consists of blue overalls, a blue apron full of pockets, and a broad flapping straw hat. More ambitious fishermen go farther afield, and with their fellow-sportsmen, the 'chasseurs,' give quite a note of colour to the drabness of the Paris termini on Sundays. Shooting has a peculiar attraction for the Parisian. Whilst there are a few well-preserved estates, such as that of the Rothschilds at Ferrières, the country as a whole is very bare of game, and shooting rights can be obtained for very little over a few fields, while perhaps a small wood can be obtained for an unimportant sum. The local butcher, baker and candlestick-maker usually combine with a few friends from Paris to rent their shooting, and tremendous are the stories that result. The well-clad shooting-party, with butts, beaters, loaders and perfectly bred and trained dogs, probably gets less out of a week on the moors than the Parisians do from their Sunday in the country, with an incredible mongrel who understands but little of what is going on, save that he is out among new and vastly interesting smells and is therefore entitled to bark and run about to his heart's content. Their game-bags are never fuller than they are just before the *casse croûte*. Out of them, long before midday, comes a succulent selection of sausages, of garlic-perfumed *paté*, crisp golden bread, and a bottle or two of the 'jolly little white wine of the country.'

Game is scarce, and the lack of protection given to bird-life would make Viscount Grey greyer. The guns blaze away at everything that creeps, crawls, runs or flies. Larks unfortunately, on account of their gastronomical qualities, are not immune, and a singular device called the *Miroir* is used to attract them to the guns. It consists of a large shiny bit of tin, shaped rather like an aeroplane propeller, which by rope is made to whirl around. The flash of it in the sunshine will bring larks from the highest heavens within range of the waiting guns. Another somewhat similar contraption, called the *Grand Duc* for mysterious reasons, is formed by a large and rough dummy owl mounted on a swivel. When moved about, it is sufficiently strange and lifelike to attract the attention of hawks or other birds of prey that may be in the neighbourhood. They swoop down upon it and, within a few yards of their prey, in panic check their flight, and fluttering in their desperate attempt to backwater are an easy mark. Rabbit is the chief bag, however, and if at the end of a long day in the open M. Dupont returns to Paris with a hare, or, rarer still, a pheasant, in his bag his sportsman's pride will overcome his sense of thrift. He will gladly and proudly declare it to the *octroi*, and at home will recount with pride the mixture of skill and intrepidity which enabled him to get it.

It is Parisians of another sort who support the many excellent golf-courses round the city, for golf in France, in spite of the many good French players, remains an expensive and exotic amusement. Most of the playing members of Chantilly, Fontainebleau, St.-Cloud, St.-Germain and La Boulie are British or American. Tennis, however, under the vigorous impulse of national successes, is making great strides, and now that the fortifications are to make way in great part for playing-fields it is certain that the requirements of the growing numbers of tennis-players will be borne in mind in the carrying out of the new gardens, for as things are at present the number of available courts inside Paris is quite inadequate to meet the demand.

THE LUXURY OF PARIS

'THERE IS SUCH AN EXCESS OF LUXURY THAT ANYONE WHO WANTED to enrich three hundred bankrupt towns need only destroy Paris. Here are endless glittering shops, which sell nothing except what is useless.'

Paris merits this description now as much as she did when it was written. Louis XIV then was sitting, or rather shining, upon the throne. He was out at Versailles, for in those days it was dowdy for a king to live in his capital. He was busy being grand in all sorts of new ways, and wanted to build for himself, and to invent methods of being remote but visible, terrible but adorable, like the sun. Hence the 'Sun-King,' the logical product of his ancestors; hence the loose necklace of palaces round the thin throat of Paris—a chain of splendour-factories in the days when splendour was an industry.

Paris had always been loved, but not always for the same reasons. Julian loved her for her quiet, provincial, virtuous life; she was such a delicious change after Rome; a haunt of ancient peace; a place where a man might rule, and yet have time to think long and well of what a pale Galilean had said four hundred years before, in another outpost of Rome, much further east of the Seven Hills than Lutetia is west of them.

After Julian came fierce, strong kings, hairy and horned, who wanted Paris as a gage of power; soldiers who fought for her as a sign of prowess; more kings; ambitious churchmen unable to rest in Sens, their Canterbury, because they wanted Paris, their London; and then those terrible politicians of old days, those exploiters of battle-fields, who bartered devastation and auctioned despair. Those gleaners of the night were sometimes sovereigns, sometimes prelates, sometimes ministers, but always rulers; and although they declared a war quite as often as they signed a peace (and it was usually a plumbers' peace, liable to produce more trouble), it is an undoubted fact that Paris managed to achieve a stormy but continuous civic existence under them.

Like all intelligent scholars, she was willing to be humble at first. She had been notable for cookery and clothing among her northern and western neighbours for a long time; but when Francis I went away a soldier and came back an artist, and the same land-change

179

was visible even in the stern Constable de Montmorency, France sat up and asked for more. Here was something new to learn, and the Hyperboreans could be told it afterwards, but she must at once know what all this meant. Why were fortresses being mixed with pleasure-galleries and fountains? What was this notion of chairs in which it was comfortable to sit, instead of the parrot-perches of tradition, and the uncomfortable alternative of session on the floor, even for ladies of the Court? This man Da Vinci at Chantilly – did you ever see anything more heady than his drawings, more irresistibly real and moving? Is it true that the Pope has a cook who knows such wonderful new dishes that Leo himself, after one Lenten soup, dubbed him 'Carême'? Are these new open-work materials ever going to be less expensive, so that longing ladies as well as kings and princes may wear lace?

The Parisian found himself in a state of flux. He was used to taking what Rome sent him – roads, soldiers, Emperors, Crucifixions, Popes, students; but now he found his furniture, his food, his thought, his art, his reading, his clothing and his daily habits utterly changed by all that came along that ancient highway. Even his cooking-pots had new-fangled shapes, and the good warm smell of ginger had vanished from the comforting steams of his kitchen, never to return. It had floated across the Channel to the barbarian English.

A hundred years after the Renaissance, France was thoroughly Italianate. She had learned much about food and clothing, and a very great deal about poisons, from her imported queens; she had been worked to a pretty point of xenophobia by Italian ministers; her method of speaking French had become lisping because of the general influx of Italians of all ranks and professions; and, or but, she had begun to feel that what she had learned in suffering she might tell in song – in other words, that it was time not only to make things for herself, but also to sell them to others.

While the Court invented palaces and festivals, Paris began to think of using throughout Europe her ability to furnish everything from a king's throne to a merry mask. She also began to think of new and witty ways of disguising, or dressing, or ornamenting everything from a comb to a cornice. 'L'article de Paris' was born under Louis XIV, and the 'glittering shops' of inutilities which characterized her then are essentially unchanged to-day. They glitter now with electricity instead of candle-flame, they sell dolls which shield telephones with their skirts, and many a true-born Parisian labours in Paris to make Chinese lacquer caparisons for wireless sets; but nothing save time has altered — they were busy hand-painting playing-cards for Madame de Pompadour then, as they are busy inlaying gramophone cabinets now.

In this infancy of the luxury trade, the dealer of the mid-seventeenth century had one or two signal advantages. For instance, he had French porcelain and French gold brocade to play with. We have nothing more amusing as novelties than galalith and vegetable silk, both very nice, very pretty, very useful, even very necessary — adjectives amounting in the long run to saying that these commodities, like really good women, are 'worthy.' But one could not run mad about them as one ran mad about the royally-patronized soft-paste porcelain, made of French earth by French potters in the Royal Factory; or as one ran mad about the product of French looms, replacing Italian and Chinese silks, and now, in the old age of Henri Quatre's grandson, justifying that Gascon monarch's energy, not only in planting mulberry trees in the Tuileries, in the very teeth of his angry Sully, but in refusing admittance to France of all foreign silks just as soon as the mulberries and the silkworms had settled comfortably down into French soil.

Henri Quatre had also brought a couple of hundred Italian weavers to Paris, and housed them in a particularly rat-ridden and miserable remnant of an abandoned palace, because he thought France should make her own gold and silver tissue. Here again his grandson, and his grandson's subjects, benefited. Could a Sun-King reign without such tissues?

'Harry of Navarre' was known as a great soldier and a great lover; he was also a great commercial traveller for his country, of the kind which sits in his office looking at foreign samples and offering prizes and help for any home-producer who will turn out stuff as good. His commercial patriotism, which is a respectable patriotism, was dropped by his peevish son, and encouraged by his magnificent grandson; for the seed had sprouted in the intermediate years, and Paris was beginning to be a Paris worthy of a Sun-King.

She had enthusiasms. In ships with high, gilded poops, merchants had brought home from strange countries of yellow men and tame monkeys huge baskets containing translucent and finely-painted 'china.' Frenchmen were hard at work trying to make something as resistant, as clear, as beautiful. Germans were trying too. What a race it was between Dresden and Sèvres!

Meanwhile, Honoré d'Urfé was an ambitious novelist, anxious to express all the polished amorosity and highly-finished mannerism of his time in a romance called *Astrée*. Like the latest work of the latest school of novelists, the book was no sooner a success than it was dramatized. Now the silk-weavers, very alert, were anxious to show what their silk-worms and their looms and their dyes could do; and so were the tailors who specialized in French silk; hence the actor who played the hero of *Astrée* wore a very soft, rather pale, mignonette-green silk coat — just the colour of the newest vases from China received by the King. Wonderful!

The hero of *Astrée*, which is a sentimental romance, is called Celadon. That is why collectors to this day talk of celadon as often as of reseda as a colour.

Long before Paris had begun to realize herself as a centre of trade she had begun to understand luxury. This was inevitable. The kind of person who must have silk stockings is grouped in one spot before that spot begins to make silk stockings endemic.

Fashionable follies do not change much. The whim for delicate pet dogs, which we think modern, was the subject of bitter comment before Henri III took to carrying a basket of puppies slung round his neck, even when he was in church or receiving the most solemn embassies. Mary Stuart dressed her dogs in blue velvet. Charles IX, who liked Italian greyhounds, apparently because they were difficult to keep in health, had thirty-six in his private apartments, all provided with collars of green and red velvet. When his favourite died, he had a pair of gloves made of the skin. The great Henri IV sent his pet dog, when it had been bitten by a mad one, to Dieppe for sea-bathing, which was in those pre-Pasteur days considered a good pre-ventive for rabies. The Governor was so good to the animal that Henri IV quoted the already old proverb: 'Who loves me loves my dog.' On the other hand, Agrippa d'Aubigné, Madame de Main-tenon's grandfather, a well-known Protestant and poet, addressed to the King, on finding the monarch's erstwhile favourite, 'Citron,' starving in the street, verses so bitter on 'ce loyer de la fidelité' that they were probably inspired by something more personal than the woes of a dog. By them, however, we learn that before enduring 'hunger, cold, blows, scorn and insult, the customary payment for serving Kings,' the pet dog slept upon his owner's bed, like his luxurious descendant of to-day.

Muff-dogs were in fashion centuries ago. Long before Henri III's baskets of doglets it was as possible as it is now to be startled at being barked at by one part of a woman's furs, indistinguishable from the rest. These toy-dogs were of breeds that have not survived, and were not only bred to be small, but kept smaller by being rubbed in strong spirits of wine for several days after their birth.

Their costume was a matter of much thought; but Paris had to wait till more recent days for the establishment of dogs' outfitters. Modern Paris has here and there, scattered among the jewellers who sell gems as large as scent-bottles, and the perfumers who sell scent as dear as jewels, shops where the muff-dog, the arm-dog, the bed-dog, the wrist-dog, the neck-dog, and all the other minute creatures who enjoy the courtesy-title of Dog, can be fitted with coats, vests, pyjamas, boots, collars and jewellery.

Until the War broke out, followed by the crazy quadrille of European exchanges, it was the habit of French exquisites to send their body-linen to England to be laundered. This light-hearted, almost light-headed, practice was balanced by some young English *elégants* who sent theirs to France. It was 'the thing,' and also the latest thing, which is the supreme stage of being 'the thing.'

In the sixteenth century the most pronounced coxcombs refused to wear a shirt more than once; but those who had a little more sense or rather less money sent their linen to Holland to be washed, because the water of the Dutch dunes was reputed to have special cleansing and blanching qualities.

Russian boots, of practically the same kind that we know, became the rage at one time – not for women, but for men. A complaint has come down to us that these boots, made fashionable by Henri IV when with his armies, became so much 'the thing' that the proud wearers introduced them not only to the drawing-room but to the ball-room. They were of the softest leather, and made so tight that it was necessary to soak the feet in cold water before booting oneself; but they can never have been the right accompaniment for the velvets and jewels of the contemporary ball-room.

Paris was on her way to eclipse the glories of Venice in her society and social life. While her buildings were still comfortless, their inhabitants were as glorious as the Queen of Sheba and King Solomon. The streets were unlighted, often unpaved, and had gutters running down the middle, which were the only substitutes for drains and dustmen; but the pageants which moved along them would leave breathless the Londoner of to-day, who thinks it wonderful if eight cream-coloured ponies draw the State Coach to Parliament, with the King in uniform and the Queen ablaze with diamonds. When Gabrielle d'Estrées made her entry to Paris just before Henri IV, whose Queen she hoped shortly to be, it was in a litter so glittering with pearls and jewels that the torches smoking in the dusk were quite outdone. That one instance may suffice to typify the wonders which were gathering throughout many decades in Paris. They were directed to all the five senses, and in her appeal to smell, sight, and taste she is still supreme.

'L'article de Paris' is the type of that useless object on which travellers delight to waste their money. It is something less crude than the 'souvenir' or 'Present from Margate,' and is usually adapted to purses too slender for the purchase of real present-y presents. It is sold all over the world, and its name has nothing to do with its origin, but only indicates a category – like Dutch cheese or suède leather. From its beginnings under Louis XIV till its capture of the noble Rue de Rivoli, in the latter half of the last century, it aimed more and more obviously at the foreigner and the provincial visitor. If this were not clear in the nature of the goods, it would be proclaimed by a particular set of manners belonging to these shops alone. Nowhere in Paris, where it must be admitted that foreigners are caught in many different webs all over the town — nowhere save in the Rue de Rivoli does the spider proclaim so clearly that the fly is a poor fool. Stop but for a second to admire this pretty pin, or to wonder who in the world would be willing to be found dead in that agglomeration of coloured glass, and out from the parlour dashes a black-clad spider to catch the rash fly.

The mercers of Paris were a very important corporation centuries ago, and their shops then were the direct precursors of the huge stores which now distinguish the city. They took their name from the Latin *merx*, meaning any kind of merchandise, its special application consisting in the fact that at that time nobody was allowed to sell anything he did not manufacture himself. As the result was to deprive the Parisian of everything that was not made in his region, it became necessary to create a class of traders who were allowed to sell everything but forbidden to make anything. They could, however, employ others to manufacture for them. Hence arose at once the middleman, the wholesale-retail distinction, and the commercial traveller — a powerful trio, whose business it has been ever since to create new demands by making new supplies. And of very great aid they have found the public in this uneconomic business; never was a trade surer of success since the serpent turned fruiterer.

To shop in Paris is the ambition of thousands of women the world over. The glass-roofed hives of the Galeries Lafayette, the Printemps, the Louvre, the Samaritain and the Bon Marché, are Meccas to these would-be pilgrims. And as in the one case the devout who accomplish the pilgrimage return with a green turban, so also the happy creature who reaches the Paris shop invariably goes home with a new hat; and each wears the acquisition in the delightful certainty that at the first glance every one at home will know where the wanderer has been.

The big stores of Paris are considerably more tiring, more crowded, more hustled and more unpractical than any picture-gallery in Europe, but the public finds them more interesting. You

185

may be crowded in the Louvre Museum on a Sunday, especially in the Apollo Gallery, where the jewels are, but there will never be the difficulty in arriving at the Venus of Milo or the Gioconda or the Winged Victory that there would be if these ladies were stocking-counters or bargain basements. Even the dreadfully tedious system of payment, which is more like some devil's version of 'Ducks and Drakes' than a method of barter, cannot deter the votaries from spending ardent hours at the shrine.

But there are other temples, temples floored with velvet and walled with brocade, where the tall priestesses in vestments of satin and crêpe from some unattainable China of their own (probably in the Lyons district) speak softly, and with slender fingers outline in the air the grace of the frock that is passing by. They have keen eyes, for they can see how the lines that hang so well upon a little thing sixty inches high by five through are just what are wanted by a lady who measures five-and-a-half feet by nearly two. And no prices are ever mentioned, for that would be ill-breeding in such a home of low voices and long bills.

These are the palaces of raiment. Jewellery nests in equally well-tended trees, and the windows of the Rue de la Paix are found attractive by natives of all countries. They are certainly interesting: diamonds are on sale which are almost as large and quite as ugly as arc-lights, and have for their only beauty the fact that they are worth enough money to banish starvation from the whole of France for a month; the loveliest works of the jeweller's craft are there, and some of the most ingenious. One cannot easily forget a brooch in the form of a bow of tartan, in which all the colours of the original wool were carried out in gems. Haughtily, indeed, did the emeralds and rubies carry themselves in this incongruous *service commandé*.

There was once a tiara in a window of this street of money which was typical of the Paris of tradition. It was exquisitely designed and made, and it was finished by seven spikes, consisting of large cabochon sapphires. They were so beautiful that they could have few peers, and each was ploughed into criss-cross furrows, and every furrow was full of diamonds. There could hardly be a more artful way of cramming evidence of money into a small space; of doing a thing well; of ruining a lovely object in the interests of fashion, and therefore of trade. It was typical of that Paris luxury which has spread her name throughout the world. She pampers her guests, and they return the caress with interest; and beneath the glittering welcome is her industrious life, her solid economy, her persevering business existence. But these she will never show, for why should anyone come abroad to find what they have left at home? And that one should come to Paris she is determined.

INDEX